CW01020197

CHRIS WHEELER
STOKE PARK CLUB

OFF THE BLOCK

CATEYS 2016

THE CATERER

CHRIS WHEELER

The Ginger Chef 'Served Up'

"Thank you to everyone who has helped me along the way on my culinary journey.
A very special mention and thanks to my amazing daughters, Vittoria and Vanessa."

@chefgingernut
www.chefchriswheeler.com

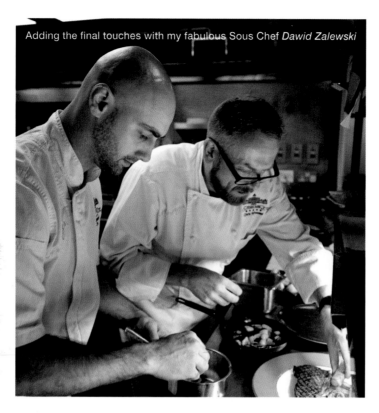
Adding the final touches with my fabulous Sous Chef *Dawid Zalewski*

CHRIS WHEELER
The Ginger Chef 'Served Up'

The last few years have been incredible for Chris Wheeler. He has recently won numerous awards including:

Hotel Chef of the Year (Over 250 Covers)
Hotel Cateys

Chef of the Year
*Berkshire and Buckinghamshire Life
Food and Drink Awards*

Fine Dining Restaurant of the Year – Humphry's
Buckinghamshire Food and Drink Awards

He has entertained the crowds on stage at the **Thame Food Festival** alongside *Raymond Blanc* and also at **Taste of London.**

And then... he made his spectacular debut on BBC2's **Great British Menu** representing the South West. Chris' appearance on the show was loved by millions of viewers and his wonderful personality shone through.

Stoke Park was also named the **'Best Gourmet Golf Resort in the World'** by *Great Golf Magazine* and Chris saw his exquisite recipes grace the pages of many a magazine, including a fabulous spread in **Hello!**

Spotting Chris' talent early on, celebrated Chef *Jean-Christophe Novelli* hired him, and Chris worked with Novelli for 12 years, becoming the youngest Sous Chef at the time to be working 7 days a week in a Michelin-starred restaurant.

Chris rose through the ranks becoming the right hand man to Jean-Christophe. The team were winning Michelin stars and 5 Red stars throughout the Novelli empire, including: *Four Seasons Park Lane, Le Provence, Lymington, Maison Novelli, Novelli EC1, Novelli W8* and *Les Saveurs,* Mayfair.

Chris still has fond memories of those days, not only because every day was different. But he also met the lady who is now his wife – Simona – at the *Four Seasons.*

Foreword by... Jean-Christophe Novelli

Chris and I go very far back, most probably 30 years by now. In fact, I remember him coming to us as a stagiaire, fresh from Bournemouth College, when I had just opened in the New Forest. I still remember so well thinking after the first evening service together that this young lad is not just talented but for sure very special. And rapidly he was able to confirm that he was effectively versatility unique. Even so, my little concern was that I didn't think he realised he was stepping onto 'Zeee unpredictable Novelli rollercoaster'. But then again, he effectively managed to spontaneously hang on very well and in fact, in 12 prolific, rewarding years working together he was clearly the one standing up proudly and comfortably on the front seat.

And I can clearly and openly state that up to today I was very fortunate to meet and work with some amazing individuals, but if it wasn't for Chris I wonder where I would have been now and for sure nowhere near as fortunate as I have been.

Chris is a mix of a very close friend and like a brother. He is simply perfect. He is genuinely hugely respected as a chef, as a manager, as a human being, as a dad and a husband; he is the perfect recipe. He is extremely strong and resistant. He is extremely kind and has an amazing sense of urgency, the perfect leader and a fabulous sense of humour. We have never had surprisingly, a single argument not even a pith.

On a daily basis, to classify him as a rock would be an insult as he is more like a mountain of titanium. And even so when the Novelli rollercoaster finally broke down and finally stopped, I remember having tears in my eyes and for sure very well, because I've only cried twice in my whole life up to today. And the reason is, early that morning I had discovered around £20,000 cash on my desk in a plastic bag and just sadly realised that Chris had quietly just remortgaged his house. Just unbelievable! I am still embarrassed and I still hate him for doing this.

Even though we have both moved in different directions in the last 15 years, I am so pleased to see he is busy riding successfully, and in his own style, his own growing rollercoaster – and for sure we all know he doesn't need anyone to teach him how to ride it.

This amazing book reflects a truly amazing chef and the perfect gentleman.

Bon appetit!

Jean-Christophe x

Chris was recently awarded *Hotel Chef of the Year* at the *Hotel Cateys*

A message from me...

Firstly I would like to thank you for buying this book - it has been a long time coming and I am delighted to be able to finally share some of my favourite recipes with you.

In this book you will find a combination of easy-to-cook recipes, some that are a little more challenging and a couple that really are show-stopping dinner party dishes!

Three ingredients that you will need handy for any recipe are; salt, pepper and olive oil. Remembering to season your food during cooking and before serving will separate bland flavours from those that will impress your diners. Always use fresh and local ingredients where possible, unless otherwise stated in the recipe.

I really want to see how you're getting on with the recipes and would love to see some photos of your dishes. Share your photos on Twitter or Instagram with **#WheeleyInspired** to share them with other budding chefs using this book!

Recipes

Starters

Wild Pollen Pan-fried Salmon with
Roasted Red Pepper Textures 21
Oven-baked Figs wrapped in Parma Ham
topped with Dorset Blue Vinny Cheese (GF) **23**
Asparagus, Toasted Rosemary and Sea Salt
Muffin with Wild Mushrooms and
Chervil Hollandaise (V) **25**
Thai Style Fishcake with Wasabi Mayonnaise,
Oriental Vegetable Salad, Dorset Ginger
and Soy Vinaigrette **27**
Tricolore Ricotta and Basil Tortellini with
Tomato Essence (V) 29
Quail, Chicken and Pistachio Terrine with Pickled
Mushrooms and Rustic Bread Crisps **31**
Dorset Crab, King Prawn and Avocado
Tian with Cucumber and Pink
Grapefruit Dressing (GF) 35
Beef Carpaccio with Roasted Figs, Fig Jelly,
Broad Bean, Rocket, Pea and Parmesan Salad **37**
Home-cured Gravadlax with a Potato and
Broad Bean Salad, Caper-berries, Caviar,
Chive and Yogurt Dressing 39
Truffle Honey Goat's Cheese with Textures
of Beetroot (GF) (V) **41**
Wild Mushroom Velouté 'Cappuccino Style'
with Cep and Dorset Sea Salt Breadsticks (V) 43
Roast Supreme of Duck with Potato Rosti,
Baby Spinach served with a Truffle Jus **45**
'Home-smoked' Pan-fried Scallops with
Salad Niçoise (GF) 47
Asparagus, Baby Courgette and Quinoa
Salad with Toasted Pumpkin Seeds and
Pomegranate Dressing (GF) (V) (DF) **49**
Warm Smoked Chicken, Watercress
and Asparagus Salad 51
Pan-fried Scallops with Celeriac Purée,
Crispy Pancetta, Caviar and Red Apple Gel **53**

Fish

Roast Fillet of Sea Bass with a Ragout
of British Clams and Mussels 59
Pan-fried Pavé of Halibut with a Butternut Squash
and Basil Risotto **61**
Roast Sea Bream with Mediterranean
Vegetables (DF) 63
Oven-baked Fillet of Cod wrapped in Pancetta
with Pomme Purée and Wild Mushroom Jus **65**
Trio of Fish 69
Pan-fried Sea Trout with Egg Noodles,
Spring Vegetables, Chilli and Saffron Sauce (DF) **71**
Posh Fish and Chips (GF) 73
Red Mullet 'Escabeche' (GF) (DF) **75**
Pavé of Sea Bass with
Fresh Asparagus (GF) (DF) 77

73

Mains

Roast Fillet of Beef with Wild Mushroom Risotto 85

Pan-fried Loin of Dorset Lamb with Mini Shepherd's Pie **87**

Roast Supreme of Chicken filled with Feta Cheese and Sun-blushed Tomatoes GF 89

Stoke Park Beef en Croute **91**

Slow-braised Lamb Shoulder GF 93

Oven-baked Pork Cutlet topped with Thinly Sliced Ham and Swiss Cheese GF **95**

Steak and Chunky Chips GF 97

Roast Loin of Venison with a Fig and Red Onion Tarte Tatin **99**

Roast Fillet of Brookfield Farm Beef with Pomme Purée 101

Roast Rump of Lamb topped with a Cranberry Crust **103**

Roast Supreme of Duck with Parsnip Purée GF 107

Roast Loin of English Veal with Watercress Purée, Oxtail and Marmite Ragout **109**

Roast Supreme of Guinea Fowl filled with Apricots GF 111

Mini Roast 'Cannon' of Beef with Mini Yorkshire Puddings **113**

Autumn Roasted Loin of Venison GF 117

Roast Lamb Cutlets with a Ragout of Peas and Beans **119**

Veal Medallions with Fondant Potatoes GF 121

Assiette of Pork **123**

Roast Mini Sirloin of Beef with 'Onion Cottage Pie' 125

Roast Supreme of Corn-fed Chicken with Sage and Onion Stuffing **127**

Pan-fried Loin of Lamb with Braised Lamb Osso Bucco 129

DIETARY KEY

 Vegan

 Vegetarian

 Gluten Free

 Dairy Free

Recipes (continued)

Vegetarian

Baked Aubergine and Mediterranean Vegetable 'Lasagne' (V) 135

Pumpkin Wellington (V) **137**

Globe Artichoke 'Tartlet' filled with Wild Mushrooms and Spinach (V) 139

Wild Mushroom Risotto with Wild Rocket (V) **141**

Double Baked Dorset Blue Vinny Cheese Soufflé (V) 143

Sun-blushed Tomato, Brie and Basil Ravioli (V) **147**

Pumpkin and Walnut Gnocchi with Pumpkin Purée, Toasted Pine Nuts and Wild Rocket (V) 149

Butternut Squash, Spinach and Vegetable Couscous filled Cannelloni (GF) (V) (DF) **151**

Truffle Macaroni Cheese Stuffed Tomato (V) 153

167

135

Desserts

Whole Baked Apple Crumble 159

Chris Wheeler's Humphry's Bar **161**

Pimm's Summer Pudding with Clotted Cream 163

Milk Chocolate and Salted Peanut Parfait **165**

Mossy's Sweet Yogurt and Coconut Mousse Dome (GF) 167

Earl Grey and Vanilla Crème Brûlée **169**

'Boodles' Tennis Ball 173

Choco Moments Crunchy Mint Biscuit and Raspberry 'Mille Feuille' **175**

Banana Rama 177

Dorset Mint Chocolate Fondant **179**

Rhubarb and Gingerbread Soufflé 181

Cherry Layered Cheesecake 'Lighthouse' **185**

Chocolate and Coffee Delice 187

Baked Pineapple Tarte Tatin with Coconut Sorbet (V) (DF) **189**

Chocolate Orange Tart with White Chocolate Ice Cream 191

STARTERS

STOKE PARK
★ ★ ★ ★ ★
COUNTRY CLUB, SPA & HOTEL

'Gourmet Golf Resort of the Year 2017'

GREAT GOLF MAGAZINE

WILD POLLEN PAN-FRIED SALMON

WITH ROASTED RED PEPPER TEXTURES, GOAT'S CURD BON BONS,
MICRO-CRESS AND MANGO GEL

 40 minutes Serves 4  Oven 180°c

Chef's comments

Adding the intensity of wild pollen to salmon really brings out the flavour – you've never tasted salmon like this before.

Ingredients

4 salmon fillets
2g wild pollen

For the pepper textures
6 red peppers
2 plum tomatoes
2 mangos
1 lemon
50ml olive oil
2g agar agar

For the bon bons
50g goat's cheese
50g flour
1 egg
2g chives (chopped)
50g breadcrumbs

For the garnish
12 small violet edible flowers
100g micro-cress

Method

Roast 2 peppers for 15 minutes, remove from the oven and wrap in cling film, allow to cool. Remove the skins and dice. Juice the remaining peppers and pass through a sieve then reduce by half by adding the agar agar. Mix and allow to set.

Blanch the tomatoes in boiling water for 30 seconds and then place into iced water to remove the skins. Quarter, remove seeds and dice.

Remove the mango skins and roughly chop. Blend until you reach a purée-like consistency.

Remove the goat's cheese skin and roll the cheese into 1cm balls – you will need 12. Roll each ball in flour, egg and then breadcrumbs, coating evenly. Heat the olive oil in a pan, add the bon bons and fry until crispy.

Season the salmon and pan-fry, skin side down for 4 minutes, sprinkle with wild pollen and pan-fry on the other side for an additional 4 minutes.

To Serve

Place the salmon in the middle of the plate, skin side down. Dot the mango and pepper purée around the plate. Mix peppers, tomatoes and chives in a pan with some olive oil, warm through and scatter on the plate. Place 3 goat's cheese bon bons on each plate and decorate with the micro-cress and flowers.

OVEN-BAKED FIGS WRAPPED IN PARMA HAM
TOPPED WITH DORSET BLUE VINNY CHEESE,
FIG OIL AND MERLOT VINEGAR DRESSING

 30 minutes    Serves 4   Oven 180°c

Chef's comments

This is a very quick and simple recipe and the creaminess of the Dorset Blue Vinny Cheese melts over the fig.

Ingredients

12 figs
6 slices of Parma ham
120g Dorset Blue Vinny Cheese
12 cherry tomatoes
200g micro-cress

For the dressing
50ml fig oil
10ml Merlot vinegar

Method

Cut each slice of Parma ham in half lengthways.

Wash the figs and make a cross on the top of each fig and push open, wrap the Parma slice around each fig, crumble 10g of Dorset Blue Vinny Cheese on top of each fig.

Whisk together the fig oil and the Merlot vinegar. Season to taste.

Place the figs on a lined baking tray, add the cherry tomatoes, season and sprinkle over some fig oil, bake in the oven for around 5 minutes or until the Dorset Blue Vinny Cheese has melted.

To Serve

Wash and spin dry the micro-leaves, mix with some dressing and place in the middle of each plate. Arrange 3 baked figs and 3 cherry tomatoes on each plate, drizzle around a little more dressing.

ASPARAGUS
SERVED ON A TOASTED ROSEMARY AND SEA SALT MUFFIN
WITH WILD MUSHROOMS AND CHERVIL HOLLANDAISE

 25 minutes   Serves 4    Oven 180°c

Chef's comments

Fond memories of PYO (Pick Your Own) at Copas Farm, asparagus is a staple of the summer vegetable season.

Ingredients

For the muffins
1 egg
125g plain flour
¼ tsp baking powder
55ml milk
40g Parmesan (grated)
Fresh rosemary (chopped)

For the wild mushrooms
200g mixed wild mushrooms
1 shallot (finely chopped)
Fresh chives (chopped)
12 asparagus spears

For the garnish
4 artichokes
Fresh chervil
200g Hollandaise sauce
Micro-cress

Method

Mix all the muffin ingredients together in a large bowl. Grease a 12-hole muffin tin and pour in the mixture. Bake for 15 minutes or until golden brown.

Cut the artichokes in half lengthways and roast in the oven until golden brown.

Meanwhile, wash the mushrooms and slice the larger ones. Pan-fry the mushrooms with the shallot in a bit of olive oil. Add the chives and season to taste.

Blanch the asparagus in boiling salted water for approximately 4 minutes before adding to the mushroom mixture.

Add the chervil to the Hollandaise sauce ready to serve.

To Serve

Place 2 slices of toasted muffin in the middle of each plate and top with 3 pieces of asparagus. Add the mushrooms on top of the asparagus and around the plate before spooning the Hollandaise sauce over the asparagus. Garnish with micro-cress.

THAI STYLE FISHCAKE

WITH WASABI MAYONNAISE, ORIENTAL VEGETABLE SALAD,
DORSET GINGER AND SOY VINAIGRETTE

 30 minutes   Serves 6 Oven 180°c

Chef's comments

Adding wasabi to mayonnaise combines the spiciness with the creaminess to tingle your taste buds.

Ingredients

For the fishcake
300g salmon & 250g cod
50g cooked white crab meat
1 stick of lemongrass
100g mashed potatoes
3 spring onions (chopped)
10g garlic (finely chopped)
1 lime
50g plain flour
2 eggs (beaten)
200g fresh breadcrumbs
5g ginger

For the vinaigrette
50ml sesame oil
25ml soy sauce
25ml Dorset Ginger drink

For the vegetable salad
1 red & yellow pepper
¼ Chinese cabbage
1 pak choi
200g beansprouts
6 baby corns
150ml mayonnaise
5g wasabi paste

Method

Halve the lemongrass and add to a pan with the fish. Cover with water, season and bring to the boil. Simmer for 6 minutes, drain and leave to cool. Remove any skin or bones, flake into a bowl and add the crab.

Sweat the spring onions, garlic and ginger in olive oil for a couple of minutes, add to the fish mixture along with the mashed potatoes.

Zest and juice the lime, add to the bowl and mix well. Divide the mixture into 6 and shape into fishcakes, dip in flour, egg and breadcrumbs.

Pan-fry on both sides until golden brown and place into the oven for 10 minutes to heat through.

To make the vinaigrette – whisk together the sesame oil, soy sauce, Dorset Ginger and season to taste.

Finely slice the baby corns, Chinese cabbage, pak choi and mixed peppers. Quickly fry in a wok and then add the beansprouts and a little vinaigrette.

Mix the wasabi paste into the mayonnaise.

To Serve

Place a large spoonful of vegetables in the middle of each plate, add the fishcake, spoon some wasabi mayonnaise around and then add the vinaigrette.

TRICOLORE RICOTTA AND BASIL TORTELLINI
WITH TOMATO ESSENCE

 60 minutes   Serves 6

Chef's comments

My wife is Italian, so when I first went to Italy, I always remember her mum making me something similar. The trick is to make sure the pasta is really thin.

Ingredients

For the tomato essence
3kg tomatoes
3 shallots
1 celery stick
2 rosemary sprigs
2 garlic cloves
1 red pepper
5g Dorset sea salt flakes
10ml honey
½ tsp Worcester Sauce
¼ tsp Tabasco

For the pasta
600g pasta flour
6g salt
6 eggs
1 tsp tomato purée
30g basil (chopped)

For the filling
50g basil (chopped)
200g ricotta

For the garnish
2 plum tomatoes
Chives (chopped)

Method

Roughly chop the tomatoes, shallots, celery, red pepper and garlic. Place into a pan and add the Dorset sea salt, honey, rosemary, Worcester sauce, Tabasco and 100ml water. Bring to the boil before removing from the heat and blending for 30 seconds. Cover and infuse for 20 minutes.

Place a muslin cloth/tea towel over a large bowl and pour the tomato mix into the cloth, tie with string and leave to drain over the bowl for 20 minutes. Once the essence is collected in the bowl, warm through in a pan (do not boil) and season to taste.

To make the pasta – use 3 separate bowls and place 200g of the flour, 2g salt and 2 eggs in each. Mix 30g basil with a little olive oil to form a paste and add this to 1 bowl. Add the tomato purée to another bowl. Separately mix the ingredients in each bowl to form 3 coloured doughs. For the filling, mix the basil with the ricotta and season to taste.

Thinly roll out each dough, keeping it covered with cling film. Cut into 6cm circles – you'll need 6 of each colour. Place the filling on one half, brush the edges with water and fold over into semicircles. Wrap around your finger to form the shape, repeat for all 18. Cook in boiling salted water for 4 minutes.

To Serve

Cut the plum tomatoes into quarters, remove seeds and finely dice, mix with the chives. Place one tortellini of each colour in the middle and sprinkle with the tomato and chives. Carefully pour over the warm tomato essence.

QUAIL, CHICKEN AND PISTACHIO TERRINE

WITH PICKLED SHIMEJI MUSHROOMS AND MADEIRA JELLY

 3.5 hours Serves 4 Oven 150°c

Chef's comments

I love this recipe because quail is not an everyday ingredient and lots of people haven't cooked with quail so it's a good challenge and an impressive dinner party dish!

Ingredients

For the terrine
2 oven-ready quail
2 chicken legs
5 thyme sprigs
3 rosemary sprigs
1 garlic clove
1 bay leaf
500ml vegetable oil
100g pistachios (peeled)
1 pack of pancetta
10g sel de rose salt (pink)
Peppercorns

For the Madeira jelly
300ml Madeira wine
3 gelatine leaves

For the pickling liquor
1 shallot
2 rosemary & thyme sprigs
1 garlic clove
80ml white wine vinegar
55g sugar
150g Shimeji mushrooms
Rustic bread crisp

Method

Place the quail, chicken, oil, thyme, rosemary, garlic, bay leaf and 5 peppercorns in an ovenproof dish. Cover with baking paper and tinfoil. Cook the meat in the oven for 2-2 ½ hours. The cooking time will depend on the size of the quail.

Meanwhile bring the vinegar, sugar, 5 peppercorns and 200ml water to the boil. Pan-fry the mushrooms with the herbs, garlic and shallot. Add to the pickling liquor and allow to cool.

For the jelly – soften the gelatine in cold water then squeeze out any excess liquid. Boil the wine, add the gelatine, whisk together, remove from the heat, pass through a sieve and leave to set.

Once cooked, remove the meat from the oil. Allow to cool before picking from the bone and removing the skin.

Blend the pistachios into a coarse dust. Divide the meat into 3 portions, season to taste. Firmly press the first layer into the mould, ensuring it is level. Sprinkle a third of the pistachios on top, covering the meat. Repeat this process twice more.

Refrigerate the terrine until firm. Trim the edges, wrap in pancetta and cling film. Steam for 7 minutes, cool. Slice as required.

To Serve

Sprinkle the pink salt across the plate, placing the terrine in the centre, cut the jelly into small cubes, drain the mushrooms and scatter both the jelly and the mushrooms around the terrine. Serve with a rustic bread crisp.

Relaxing with Ruby and Tilly

Chris joined *Stoke Park* in 2003 and for the past fifteen years he has steadily been building the club's culinary reputation.

In addition to *Humphry's* winning *3 AA Rosettes,* much praise and accolades have been attributed to Chris and his team, with *Woman and Home* magazine stating, *'Humphry's is the last word in fine dining'.*

Leading chefs have commented that *Humphry's* is *'an experience you want to relive again and again'* and *The Daily Telegraph* naming *Stoke Park* as having one of *'Britain's Best Afternoon Teas'.*

Humphry's was voted in the *'Top 20 Best out of Town Restaurants'* by *Harper's Bazaar,*

'Top 5 Out of Town Restaurants' by the *Square Meal Restaurant Guide* and Chris won *'Best Local Menu'* for his use of local produce at the *Buckinghamshire and Berkshire Life Food and Drink Awards*, and featured in *Tatler's Restaurant Guide* 2013, 2014 and again in 2016 with the editor writing in the guide that Chris had cooked *'two of the best dishes he had eaten all year!'*

Chris will always remember driving up that long drive of *Stoke Park* for his interview thinking, "this is the place for me, not only is it amazing but it also has the wow factor."

"Two of the best dishes
I had eaten all year."
TATLER RESTAURANT GUIDE

Humphry's.

DORSET
SHELLFISH

DORSET CRAB, KING PRAWN AND AVOCADO TIAN
WITH CUCUMBER AND PINK GRAPEFRUIT DRESSING

 30 minutes   Serves 6

Chef's comments

This is from my early days as a chef. This is a twist on my mentor, Jean-Christophe Novelli's, dish.

Ingredients

For the tian
1 avocado (diced)
8 cooked tiger prawns
160g white Dorset crab meat
10g caviar
10g dill (chopped)
10g chives (chopped)
10g tarragon (chopped)
½ lemon (juice only)
100g crème fraîche
4 soft boiled quail eggs
¼ cucumber

For the dressing
100ml pink grapefruit juice
100ml extra virgin olive oil

For the garnish
12 pink grapefruit segments
100g mixed salad & cress

Method

In a bowl, mix the avocado, half the lemon juice, tarragon and seasoning. Press some mixture into each tian ring ensuring they're just over a third full.

Cut the king prawns in half lengthways and place 2 halves on top of the avocado.

Mix the Dorset crab and dill together and press into the mould until nearly full.

Reduce the grapefruit juice until syrup-like, then whisk in the olive oil.

Mix the crème fraîche with the chives, seasoning and remaining lemon juice. Place on top of the crab. Allow to set in the fridge.

To Serve

Season the salad and place in the middle of the plate. Add the tian on top and remove the ring. Pour over the dressing and place 3 segments on each plate. Decorate the tian with a cucumber crown and top with the egg and caviar. Garnish with cress.

BEEF CARPACCIO

WITH ROASTED FIGS, FIG JELLY, BROAD BEAN, ROCKET, PEA AND PARMESAN SALAD

 30 minutes   Serves 4   Oven 180°c

Chef's comments

Using peas and broad beans adds a freshness and a crunch to the dish.

Ingredients

For the carpaccio
500g English beef fillet
3 tarragon sprigs
50g parsley
2 tbsp Dijon mustard

For the roasted figs
4 figs
10ml maple syrup

For the garnish
50g fig jelly
100g Parmesan (grated)
40g broad beans
40g peas
150g wild rocket
100ml Merlot vinegar
1 gelatine leaf
(soaked in cold water)
40ml olive oil
20g mixed soft herbs (chopped)

Method

Generously season the beef fillet, quickly seal in a hot pan and remove onto a plate. Chop the parsley and tarragon, brush the sealed beef fillet with the Dijon mustard and roll in the herbs, wrap in cling film and place in the fridge for at least 2 hours. Remove from the fridge, unwrap and thinly slice. Arrange 8 thin slices on the plate in a flower shape.

Line a baking tray and make 4 circles of Parmesan, cook in the oven for 3 minutes until melted. Cool for 1 minute on the tray before wrapping the circles over the base of a small cup to form a basket. Allow to cool and crisp.

Blend the olive oil with the soft herbs until the oil turns a rich green colour. Warm the Merlot vinegar in a pan and whisk in the squeezed gelatine, stir to form a vinegar gel.

Cut each fig into 4, place on a baking tray and drizzle with maple syrup, roast in the oven for 3 minutes, remove and cool. Cut the fig jelly into 16 small cubes.

To Serve

Mix the peas, broad beans and wild rocket together with a little olive oil and place into the Parmesan baskets. Arrange in the middle of the carpaccio. Decorate with figs and jelly around the plate. Garnish with vinegar gel and herb oil.

HOME-CURED GRAVADLAX

WITH A JERSEY ROYAL POTATO AND BROAD BEAN SALAD, CAPER-BERRIES, CAVIAR, CHIVE AND NATURAL GREEK YOGURT DRESSING

 4.5 hours   Serves 8

Chef's tip

The important thing is to add a little sugar to the salt when curing the gravadlax.

Ingredients

For the gravadlax
1.5kg salmon fillet (pinned & boned)
750g sea salt
75g sugar
1 litre olive oil
2 thyme sprigs
300g dill (finely chopped)
30g Dijon mustard

For the dressing
50g caviar
150ml Tims Dairy Natural Greek Yogurt

For the garnish
1kg Jersey Royal potatoes
2 shallots (finely diced)
100ml house dressing
50g chives (chopped)
100g broad beans
150g mixed baby leaves
24 caper-berries

Method

Mix the sea salt and sugar together, lay the salmon fillet in a tray skin side down and cover with the salt and sugar mixture, leave for 2 hours. Remove from the salt and wipe the salmon clean.

Place the salmon in a deep tray and cover with the oil and thyme. Leave for another 2 hours. Remove from the oil and dry the salmon. Brush with mustard and sprinkle with the dill, wrap in cling film for 10 minutes. Unwrap the salmon and using a sharp knife, slice thinly into 32 pieces.

Wash and cook the potatoes in boiling salted water for 12 minutes, drain and cool. Dice the potatoes keeping the skin on. Mix the potatoes with the diced shallots, half of the chives, half of the broad beans and the house dressing.

Mix the remaining chives with the yogurt and caviar. Season to taste.

To Serve

Place a spoonful of potato salad in the middle of each plate, arrange 4 slices of gravadlax around the potatoes, spoon the yogurt dressing around. Garnish with 3 caper-berries, baby leaves and remaining broad beans.

TRUFFLE HONEY GOAT'S CHEESE

WITH TEXTURES OF BEETROOT

 20 minutes   Serves 4

Chef's comments

The sweetness of the truffle honey assists in bringing out the flavour of the goat's cheese.

Ingredients

For the goat's cheese
200g goat's cheese
10g truffle honey
70ml double cream

For the beetroot textures
200ml fresh beetroot juice
2g agar agar
2 baby candy beetroot
2 baby golden beetroot
4 baby beetroot
1 pickled beetroot (finely diced)

For the garnish
1 large candy beetroot
8g beetroot powder
40g frisée salad

Method

Place the goat's cheese and truffle honey into a blender and season. Slowly add the double cream, blend until smooth. Peel and cook all the baby beetroot separately in boiling salted water for 6 minutes, drain and cool.

Cut the baby candy and golden beetroot into quarters and the normal ones into halves. Bring the beetroot juice to the boil, add the agar agar and stir in until cold and gel-like. Place into a squeezy-bottle.

Wash and spin dry the frisée salad. Peel and thinly slice the large candy beetroot and place into iced water.

To Serve

Make a line across each plate with beetroot powder. Using a hot spoon make 2 quenelles of goat's cheese on one side of the plate. Arrange the diced and baby beetroot around the goat's cheese, place a few drops of beetroot gel around, garnish with the salad and candy beetroot. Drizzle olive oil over the salad.

WILD MUSHROOM VELOUTÉ 'CAPPUCCINO STYLE'
WITH CEP AND DORSET SEA SALT BREADSTICKS

 60 minutes   Serves 10   Oven 200°c

Chef's comments

This is the easiest dish to prepare in the book and by simply adding the cappuccino effect. It really creates a wow factor.

Ingredients

For the breadsticks

400ml warm water

40g sugar

20g fresh yeast

3 tbsp butter (melted)

675g strong flour

½ tsp of table salt

1 egg

10ml milk

35g Dorset sea salt flakes

10g cep powder

For the soup

1kg mixed wild mushrooms

2 onions

1 leek

2 garlic cloves

50g dried cep mushrooms

50ml white wine

4 litres of mushroom
or vegetable stock

2 rosemary sprigs

2 thyme sprigs

150ml double cream

200ml milk (for froth)

5g cep powder

Method

Dissolve the yeast in warm water. Mix the flour, sugar and salt into a bowl, slowly add the melted butter and yeast mixture. Mix well and leave to prove in a warm place for approximately 30 minutes.

Knead and roll into long thin sticks before placing on a lined tray. You need 4 per person. Mix the egg with the milk and brush onto the breadsticks. Sprinkle with the salt flakes and cep powder. Bake for 12 minutes until golden brown. Remove and allow to cool.

To make the soup – heat the stock in a saucepan and add the dried cep mushrooms, leave to simmer. Peel and slice the onion and garlic, sweat in a large pan, wash and slice the leek add to the pan, sweat for 2 minutes, add the rosemary and thyme.

Wash and slice the wild mushrooms, add to the pan and sweat for 2 minutes before adding the wine and stock. Cook for 30 minutes and then blend until smooth. Pass through a sieve and check seasoning, whisk in the double cream.

To Serve

Divide the soup between 10 soup cups/mugs. Froth the milk into a foam and place on top of the soup. Sprinkle with the cep powder to give a cappuccino effect. Serve with 4 breadsticks each.

ROAST SUPREME OF DUCK

WITH POTATO ROSTI AND BABY SPINACH SERVED WITH A TRUFFLE JUS

 30 minutes   Serves 4   Oven 180°c

Chef's comments

In this recipe we are using quince jelly which is traditionally used with cheese but I find it brings out the flavour of the duck.

Ingredients

2 duck breasts

For the potato rosti
2 Maris Piper potatoes
30g butter

For the garnish
40g quince jelly
5g black truffle shavings/oil
100ml red wine jus
Rosemary
200g baby spinach

Method

Seal the duck breasts on both sides. Roast in the oven for 3-4 minutes on each side with some rosemary. Once cooked, leave to rest for 5 minutes.

Melt the butter and set aside. Meanwhile peel, wash and grate the potatoes, then squeeze the grated potato dry using a tea towel. Place into a bowl, add the melted butter and season.

Shape the potato mixture into 4 rounds and shallow-fry the potatoes for 4 minutes on each side, until golden brown.

Wash the baby spinach and sauté in a little olive oil, drain well.

Cut the quince jelly into 12 cubes (roughly 1cm each). Warm the red wine jus and add the truffle shaving or oil. Slice each duck breast into 8 slices.

To Serve

Place a potato rosti in the middle of each plate, add some baby spinach on top, then top with 4 slices of duck. Arrange 3 cubes of quince jelly around, pour the red wine truffle jus around.

'HOME-SMOKED' PAN-FRIED SCALLOPS

SERVED WITH A SALAD NIÇOISE

 30 minutes Serves 4

Chef's comments

This dish is more complex and requires a significant amount of effort – but the end result is worth it.

Ingredients

12 scallops

For the dressing
Chives (finely chopped)
100ml natural thick yogurt

For the salad
8 cherry tomatoes (halved)
100g green beans (blanched)
Mixed peppers
(¼ of each colour cut into diamonds)
4 new potatoes
(sliced & blanched)
8 black pitted olives
8 caper-berries
200g mixed leaf salad
(including watercress)
4 quail eggs (soft boiled)

Method

In a warm pan, place the potato, cherry tomatoes, mixed peppers, olives, caper-berries and green beans along with some olive oil.

Heat thoroughly allowing to colour lightly. Take off the heat once ready and keep to one side.

In a non-stick pan, sear the scallops on both sides, allowing them to become a nice golden brown colour. Drop a knob of butter into the pan just before finishing.

For the dressing – combine the chives with the natural yogurt and season to taste.

To Serve

Place the dressed salad leaves into the bowl, arrange your beans, potatoes, olives, caper-berries, peppers and tomatoes around the plate. Place the seared scallops on top. Garnish with the quail eggs, natural yogurt and chive dressing.

To smoke – place the glass dome on top of plate, place the tube inside and smoke for a few minutes.

On serving, to create a sensation, remove the dome in front of guests at the table!

ASPARAGUS, BABY COURGETTE AND QUINOA SALAD

WITH TOASTED PUMPKIN SEEDS AND POMEGRANATE DRESSING

 30 minutes   Serves 4

Chef's comments

Superfood salads are a great way to have a filling yet nutritious meal. This dish caters for people with all allergies.

Ingredients

24 asparagus spears
12 baby courgettes
8 baby golden beetroot
1 broccoli
8 baby corns
400g baby mixed salad
40g pumpkin seeds
200g gluten-free quinoa
Mixed peppers (¼ of each)

For the dressing
1 pomegranate
100ml extra virgin oil olive
10ml Merlot vinegar

Method

Remove all seeds from the pomegranate over a bowl, ensuring to keep the juice. Add the seeds to the bowl with the Merlot vinegar and whisk in 90ml of olive oil. Season to taste.

Finely dice the peppers and place into a pan with the quinoa. Cover with water, season and bring to the boil. Simmer for 8 minutes then drain.

Cut the baby courgettes and baby corns in half lengthways and chargrill on both sides until soft. Roughly 1 minute on each side.

Blanch the asparagus in boiling salted water for 4 minutes, drain. Peel and cook the baby beetroot in boiling salted water for 5 minutes and cut in half.

Cut the broccoli into small pieces, blanch in boiling salted water for 2 minutes, drain.

Wash and spin dry the baby salad leaves. Toast the pumpkin seeds under the grill for a few minutes until they start to colour.

To Serve

Mix the salad, quinoa and vegetables together, add some dressing, mix well and arrange on each plate. Sprinkle over some toasted pumpkin seeds. Drizzle over more dressing and some olive oil.

WARM SMOKED CHICKEN, WATERCRESS AND ASPARAGUS SALAD
WITH A POACHED EGG AND A ROSE HARISSA NATURAL YOGURT DRESSING

 20 minutes   Serves 8   Oven 180°c

Chef's comments

Very simple, healthy and using natural yogurt spiced up with Rose Harissa makes the ideal zingy dressing.

Ingredients

4 cooked smoked chicken breasts
24 asparagus spears
8 poached eggs
600g watercress

For the dressing
400ml Tims Dairy Low
Fat Natural Yogurt
2 tbsp Rose Harissa

Method

Pan-fry the smoked chicken breasts on both sides and place in the oven for 10 minutes to warm through. Remove from the oven and slice each chicken breast into 10.

Cook the asparagus for 4 minutes in boiling salted water, drain and toss in olive oil.

Mix the Rose Harissa and low fat natural yogurt together.

Place the poached eggs into boiling water for 2 minutes, once they are hot, drain.

Wash and spin the watercress, season with a little olive oil.

To Serve

Place a handful of watercress in the middle of each bowl, add 3 pieces of asparagus on top, arrange 5 slices of chicken on top, skin side up. Place a poached egg on top and pour over the Rose Harissa and natural yogurt dressing, garnish with watercress.

PAN-FRIED SCALLOPS

WITH CELERIAC PURÉE, CRISPY PANCETTA, PORT REDUCTION AND CAVIAR

 25 minutes   Serves 4    Oven 180°c

Chef's comments

The secret to cooking scallops is to quickly seal on both sides and not to overcook. Scallops always seem intimidating to cook at home but they're actually really quick and easy!

Ingredients

12 large scallops

For the purée
1 celeriac
150ml milk

For the garnish
200ml port
8 slices of pancetta
10g caviar

Method

Peel and chop the celeriac into cubes – roughly 1cm square and then add to a saucepan with the milk and some salt. Cook until soft.

Drain the celeriac and blend until smooth (add some of the cooking liquid if necessary to create a smooth consistency).

Bring the port to the boil in a saucepan and reduce to a syrup, leave to cool. Pour into a squeezy-bottle if you have one.

Place the pancetta between 2 sheets of greaseproof paper on a baking tray, weigh down with another tray to keep the pancetta flat. Cook in the oven for 15 minutes or until light brown in colour. Leave to cool and crisp up.

Season and cook the scallops in a hot non-stick pan with a little olive oil until golden brown, approximately 1-2 minutes on each side.

To Serve

Create a zig-zag pattern on each plate using the port reduction. Make 3 small mounds of celeriac purée on each plate and place a scallop on top of each mound. Add a slice of crispy pancetta to the 2 end scallops of each plate and place ¼ of the caviar on the middle scallop.

FISH

In 2018 whilst continuing heading up the kitchens at *Stoke Park,* Chris started his consultancy and was appointed by *Lamb and Wolf Ltd* to advise on their chain of pubs and restaurants in Dorset – *The Nothe Tavern & Kings Arms* in Weymouth and *The Angel* in Poole.

Originally from Swanage in Dorset, where his parents still live, Chris' passion, enthusiasm and culinary excellence was spotted and nurtured from a young age.

While at *The Purbeck School* in Wareham, Dorset, he grew to love home economics with the help of his cookery teacher 'Betty' who he still remains friends with. She encouraged him to join the *Bournemouth and Poole College* where he studied a Chef Diploma Course in *Kitchen and Patisserie.*

Whilst studying he worked at the *Grand Hotel* in Swanage before his course took him to the *Domaine De Bassible Hotel* and Michelin-starred restaurant located in the cosy French town of Ségos, which fed the rising stars' ability and made him fall in love with food.

A fantastic day on the boat fishing with my friends from Dorset Shellfish

ROAST FILLET OF SEA BASS

WITH A RAGOUT OF BRITISH CLAMS AND MUSSELS, SAMPHIRE AND DORSET BLACK COW VODKA CREAM SAUCE

 45 minutes   Serves 4

Chef's comments

This dish reminds me of living by the sea and also of the times when I'm down in Weymouth consulting at The Nothe Tavern.

Ingredients

4 sea bass fillets
400g Thai/regular asparagus
200g spinach
200g pomme purée (mashed potatoes)

For the mussels
100g clams
100g mussels
40g shallots (finely chopped)
10g chives (finely chopped)
20ml white wine

For the sauce
200ml fish stock
200ml white wine
100ml double cream
20ml Black Cow vodka
1 small onion (diced)
1 small leek (diced)
1 celery stick (diced)

For the garnish
Micro-cress

Method

Make the sauce by sweating the diced onion, leek and celery with a little olive oil and the white wine. Reduce by half. Add the fish stock and reduce again by half. Stir in the double cream, Black Cow vodka and season. Simmer for 5 minutes.

Season the sea bass and pan-fry for roughly 3 minutes on each side. Wash the spinach and sweat in a pan with a little butter. Blanch the asparagus for 30 seconds in boiling salted water and add to the sea bass.

Sweat the finely diced shallots in a saucepan, add the clams and mussels, cover with a lid for 1 minute. Add the white wine and cover again for 2 minutes or until all the clams and mussels are open. Add the chives.

To Serve

Place a portion of pomme purée in the middle of each plate, topping with spinach and asparagus. Serve the sea bass on top, skin side up. Dot the mussels and clams around the outside and spoon the sauce over the top and garnish with micro-cress.

CREED
THE FOODSERVICE COMPANY

PAN-FRIED PAVÉ OF HALIBUT

WITH A LEEK, BUTTERNUT SQUASH AND BASIL RISOTTO

 45 minutes   Serves 4   Oven 180°c

Chef's comments

This is a very summery dish in which the light risotto complements the flavours of the delicate halibut.

Ingredients

4 halibut fillets
4 marinated artichokes
Basil, rosemary, chives
1 butternut squash
2 garlic cloves

For the risotto
60ml white wine
250ml vegetable stock
100g Parmesan (grated)
150g risotto rice
20g butter (diced)
10g mascarpone
50g peas
1 shallot (finely diced)
1 large leek (finely chopped)

For the sauce
100ml fish stock
1 onion (finely diced)
25ml double cream

Method

Peel and de-seed the butternut squash and cut into 1cm cubes, keeping the trimmings for later. Roast in the oven until soft with some olive oil, rosemary and garlic.

Meanwhile, in a saucepan sweat the diced shallot and leek with some olive oil, add the risotto rice and season. Add 30ml of the wine, slowly adding the hot vegetable stock – a small amount at a time until the risotto is just cooked.

Add the peas, roasted butternut squash and stir. Fold in the butter, Parmesan, mascarpone and basil.

To make the sauce – sweat the diced onion and the butternut squash trimmings with a little olive oil in a pan. Add the remaining 30ml of wine and reduce by half.

Add the fish stock and reduce again by half. Once reduced, stir in the double cream and season. Simmer for 5 minutes then blend. Pass through a sieve, finely chop the chives and add.

Cut the artichokes in half lengthways and roast until golden brown. Season the halibut fillets and pan-fry on both sides until golden brown, transfer to the oven for 5 minutes.

To Serve

Place a portion of risotto on each plate, placing the halibut on top. Add 2 artichoke halves, spoon around the sauce and garnish with chives.

ROAST SEA BREAM

WITH MEDITERRANEAN VEGETABLES,
CRUSHED NEW POTATOES AND TOMATO PROVENÇALE SAUCE

 45 minutes   Serves 4   Oven 160°c

Chef's tip

Always cook sea bream skin side down first to achieve a crispy skin and soft fish.

Ingredients

4 sea bream fillets

For the vegetables
2 red peppers
4 baby aubergines
8 baby courgettes
800g new potatoes (peeled and cooked)

For the sauce
500g plum tomatoes (finely chopped)
1 red onion (finely sliced)
2 garlic cloves (finely sliced)
2 thyme & rosemary sprigs
200ml tomato juice
2 basil sprigs (chopped)

Method

Cut the peppers in half lengthways, leaving the stalk on and remove the seeds. Cut the baby aubergines and courgettes in half lengthways. Divide the aubergines and courgettes into 4 and place inside each red pepper half.

Place on a baking tray, season and add a drizzle of olive oil, 1 sprig of thyme and rosemary and cook for 10 minutes (until all the vegetables are soft).

Crush the new potatoes, season and place into the oven for 8 minutes until they start to brown.

Sweat the finely diced onion and garlic in a pan, chop the remaining rosemary and thyme and add to the pan, mix well. Add the tomato, season and sweat for a couple of minutes, add the tomato juice and simmer for 5 minutes. Add the basil just before serving.

Score the skin side of each sea bream, pan-fry in some olive oil skin side down for 3 minutes before turning for a further 3 minutes.

To Serve

Place a ¼ of the crushed potatoes in the middle of each plate, topping with a stuffed pepper half. Place the fillet of sea bream on top and pour the tomato provençale sauce around.

OVEN-BAKED COD WRAPPED IN PANCETTA

WITH POMME PURÉE AND WILD MUSHROOM JUS

 40 minutes    Serves 4   Oven 180°c

Chef's comments

Mushroom jus seems like an unusual pairing with the cod but due to the fact it's wrapped in pancetta it brings all the flavours together.

Ingredients

4 cod loins
200g sliced pancetta
400g spinach
600g pomme purée
10ml milk

For the sauce
400g mixed wild mushrooms
1 shallot (finely diced)
100ml mushroom stock
300ml red wine jus

For the garnish
Pea shoots (1 pack)

Method

Place 5 slices of pancetta on a sheet of cling film and place a piece of cod on top. Carefully roll up, repeat this with the other 3 pieces of cod. Remove the cling film and pan-fry the cod on both sides and then place in the oven for 10 minutes.

Wash the wild mushrooms and cut the bigger ones in half. Sauté in olive oil with the diced shallot and season.

Remove from the pan and add the mushroom stock, reduce by half and then add the red wine jus, bring to the boil and then add the mushrooms back to the pan.

Wash the spinach and sauté in a little butter, season and drain well. Heat up the pomme purée (mashed potato) in a pan with the milk.

To Serve

Place a spoonful of pomme purée in the middle of the plate, add some spinach and then top with the baked wrapped cod, pour the mushroom jus over and garnish with pea shoots.

TRIO OF FISH

SEA BREAM WITH ASPARAGUS HOLLANDAISE, RED MULLET WITH SAFFRON RISOTTO
AND SEA BASS WITH BABY MEDITERRANEAN VEGETABLES

 45 minutes   Serves 6   Oven 180°c

Chef's comments

This dish showcases a sample of the wide range of fish from my friends at Kingfisher Brixham.

Ingredients

For the sea bream

2 sea bream fillets
18 asparagus tips
60ml Hollandaise sauce
1 spring onion
50ml extra virgin olive oil

For the red mullet

3 red mullet fillets
120g risotto rice
1 onion
240ml vegetable stock
10ml white wine
5g saffron

For the sea bass

2 sea bass fillets
6 baby red peppers
3 baby courgettes
3 baby aubergines
150g cherry tomatoes
1 shallot
1 thyme sprig
1 rosemary sprig
1 garlic clove
½ tsp honey

Method

Peel and cook the asparagus in boiling salted water for 4 minutes, drain and toss in olive oil. Thinly slice the spring onion and add the extra virgin olive oil, infuse for 20 minutes.

Heat the stock, peel and finely slice the onion, sweat in a saucepan. Add the saffron and rice, mix well, add the white wine and cook for 2 minutes. Slowly add the vegetable stock to the rice and keep stirring. Cook for 15 minutes or until soft.

Cut the baby peppers in half lengthways, leaving the stalk on and remove the seeds. Cut the baby aubergines and courgettes in half lengthways, place all the baby vegetables on a baking tray, season, add a drizzle of oil, thyme and rosemary. Cook for 10 minutes (until all the vegetables are soft).

Slice the shallot and garlic, sweat in a saucepan with the rosemary, cut the cherry tomatoes in half and add to the pan, cook for 5 minutes, add the honey and then blend, pass through a sieve into a pan.

Cut the red mullet fillets in half and the sea bream and sea bass into thirds. Pan-fry the fish in olive oil for a couple of minutes skin side down, turn over and cook for another couple of minutes.

To Serve

Place 3 asparagus tips at one end of each plate, pour over some Hollandaise sauce. Top with a piece of sea bream and drizzle with spring onion oil. Spoon some saffron risotto on the middle of the plate and top with red mullet. Arrange 2 halves of red pepper, ½ aubergine and ½ baby courgette at the other end of the plate and place a piece of sea bass on top, pour some tomato liquid around.

PAN-FRIED SEA TROUT

WITH EGG NOODLES, SPRING VEGETABLES, CHILLI AND SAFFRON BROTH

DF

 40 minutes   Serves 4

Chef's comments

While I was travelling in Asia I loved their flavour combinations which I have recreated in this dish. The sea trout is a very light fish and the broth isn't too overpowering.

Ingredients

4 portions of sea trout
400g egg noodles
1 yellow & green courgette
2 carrots
100g mange tout

For the broth

400ml fish stock
2 spring onions
1 red chilli
1 small piece of ginger
4 coriander sprigs
Pinch of saffron

Method

Pan-fry the sea trout for 4 minutes on both sides. Blanch the egg noodles in boiling salted water and drain.

Place the fish stock and saffron in a pan and bring to the boil. Slice the ginger, spring onions and chilli and add to the pan, simmer for 1 minute.

Cut the courgettes, carrots and mange tout into julienne (long very thin strips) and add to the pan, add the egg noodles and mix well, finely chop the coriander and add to the pan.

To Serve

Using a roasting fork or tongs place a pile of the egg noodles and vegetable mixture in the middle of each bowl, place the sea trout on top and pour the broth around.

POSH 'FISH AND CHIPS'

PAN-FRIED JOHN DORY WITH FONDANT POTATOES, PEA SHOOTS, PEA SAUCE AND LEMON VINEGAR

 45 minutes   Serves 6   Oven 180°c

Chef's comments

Since I come from a seaside town, Swanage, I love fish and chips. Here I have given it a little modern twist.

Ingredients

6 John Dory fillets (halved)
300g samphire

For the potatoes
6 large red-skinned potatoes
500ml vegetable stock
50g butter

For the dressings
500g peas
1 onion
1 mint sprig
2 lemons (zested and juiced)
20ml white wine vinegar

For the garnish
Pea shoots (1 pack)

Method

Peel the potatoes and cut each potato into a circle using a cutter, then slice each circle in half to produce 2 slices from each potato, pan-fry each potato circle in a little oil. Place in an ovenproof dish and add the butter and half the vegetable stock – cover and cook for 20 minutes. The potatoes should be golden brown and soft in the middle.

Place the lemon zest and juice into a pan, add the vinegar and reduce to a syrup.

Peel and slice the onion, sweat in a saucepan with half the peas. Season and add the remaining vegetable stock. Bring to the boil, blend and pass through a sieve.

Sweat the remaining peas in a pan, finely chop the mint and add to the pan.

Pan-fry the John Dory fillets in olive oil for a couple of minutes skin side down, turn over and cook for another couple of minutes. When you turn the fish add the samphire to the pan and sweat.

To Serve

Place 1 potato ring in the middle of the plate, top with 1 John Dory fillet and some samphire and then add 1 more potato ring and finish with the John Dory fillet skin side up. Pour some pea sauce around and sprinkle the peas around, add a few drops of the lemon vinegar syrup and garnish with the pea shoots.

RED MULLET 'ESCABECHE'

WITH FENNEL AND BABY BEETROOT

 40 minutes Serves 4

Chef's comments

Red mullet isn't the most obvious choice for a fish dish but it should be available from your local fishmongers or supermarket. The escabeche just adds a light spice.

Ingredients

8 red mullet fillets
(scaled, pinned and boned)

For the escabeche

500ml vegetable stock
150ml white wine
5g saffron
2 oranges (zested and juiced)
4 cardamom seeds
2 garlic cloves
2 onions
2 red & yellow peppers
4 carrots
2 celery sticks
2 thyme sprigs
Tabasco & Worcestershire sauce
100ml tomato juice

For the garnish

8 baby fennel
8 baby golden beetroot
4 baby beetroot (halved)
20g samphire

Method

Peel and finely slice the onions, celery, carrots and garlic. Sweat in a saucepan with the cardamom seeds, thyme, saffron and seasoning. Slice all the peppers and add the white wine and reduce by half. Pour the orange zest and juice into the pan. Add the vegetable stock and reduce by half again, add the tomato juice and a little Tabasco and Worcestershire sauce. Cook for a couple of minutes.

Peel and cook the baby beetroot in boiling salted water (cook the golden ones first) drain and toss in a little olive oil and season.

Blanch the baby fennel. Pan-fry the red mullet fillets in olive oil, skin side down first and cook for a couple of minutes on both sides. Then add the baby fennel to colour on both sides and toss the samphire in the pan.

To Serve

Place a large spoonful of the escabeche mixture including the juice in the middle of the plate, place 1 fillet of red mullet skin side up, then place 1 baby fennel and add another red mullet fillet, arrange the baby beetroot around and top with samphire.

PAVÉ OF SEA BASS

WITH A SUMMER VEGETABLE SALAD

 45 minutes   Serves 4   Oven 170°c

Chef's comments

This is a very summery and colourful dish.

Ingredients

4 wild sea bass fillets

For the salad

16 asparagus spears
100g small wild mushrooms
Pea shoots (1 pack)
1 radish bunch
8 sun-blushed tomatoes
40g peas
½ red pepper
100g mixed baby summer leaves
2 dill sprigs

For the dressing

100ml extra virgin olive oil
8 spring onions

Method

Score the skin side of each wild sea bass and pan-fry in some olive oil skin side down for 5 minutes before turning for a further 4 minutes.

Cook the asparagus in boiling salted water for 4 minutes, and cut 4 pieces in half lengthways. Dice the red pepper and sweat in a little oil for 1 minute before adding the asparagus.

Wash and spin dry the summer leaves. Blanch the peas for 1 minute in boiling water. Wash and sauté the wild mushrooms in olive oil for 2 minutes. Wash and cut each radish into 4 wedges.

Finely slice the spring onions, season and mix with the extra virgin olive oil.

To Serve

Place 3 pieces of whole asparagus in the middle of the plate, place the cooked sea bass on top. On one side of the plate add some mixed summer leaves, 2 asparagus halves, a few wild mushrooms, peas, radishes, diced red pepper and sun-blushed tomatoes. Drizzle the spring onion oil and garnish with the pea shoots and dill.

My fabulous brigade at Stoke Park:

(Left to right) Dawid Zalewski, Przemyslaw Pyrka (Chips), Natali Lyubenova, Tom Addy, Me, Craig Smith, Levente Torok and Adam Kapala

MAINS

In 2017 Chris was invited to be the **UK Ambassador** for *Quality Standard Mark Beef and Lamb* and has become a *Patron of the East Berkshire College Hospitality and Catering Academy* alongside fellow *Chef Tom Kerridge.* He was back at the *Thame Food Festival* entertaining the crowds and travelled the country promoting *Quality Standard Mark Beef and Lamb,* as well as wowing guests at **Stoke Park.**

In 2018, Chris was invited to continue being the *UK Ambassador* for *QSM Beef and Lamb* which had already seen him travel all over the country and produce two amazing *'Off the Block'* videos showcasing some of his favourite beef and lamb dishes.

ROAST FILLET OF BEEF

WITH WILD MUSHROOM RISOTTO, BABY TURNIPS AND RED WINE JUS

 40 minutes   Serves 4   Oven 180°c

Chef's comments

This is mixing my wife's favourite ingredient – risotto, with my favourite ingredient – steak.

Ingredients

4 beef fillets (6oz each)

For the risotto

200g risotto rice

1 litre of mushroom stock

250ml white wine

1 shallot (finely diced)

50g Parmesan (grated)

20g butter

200g mixed wild mushrooms

For the garnish

12 baby turnips

12 baby cep mushrooms

100g wild rocket

150ml red wine jus

5g sugar

Method

Cook the shallot in a saucepan with a little oil. Add the risotto rice and season. Pour in the white wine and slowly add the warm mushroom stock. Keep stirring for around 20 minutes, adding more stock as needed until the risotto is cooked.

Sauté the mixed wild mushrooms in a hot pan, season to taste. Add ¾ of the mushrooms to the risotto, keeping behind ¼ for the garnish. Check the seasoning and add the Parmesan and butter. Stir well.

Season and seal the beef. Oven cook for approximately 6 minutes for medium rare, cooking longer for different preferences.

Peel the turnips and place them in a saucepan with cold water, add a little salt and sugar. Bring to the boil and simmer for 10 minutes until the baby turnips become soft. Drain and toss in olive oil and season to taste. Wash and pan-fry the cep mushrooms in a little olive oil until soft. Season to taste.

Deep-fry the wild rocket in a little oil in a fryer for approximately 15 seconds until the rocket becomes crispy. Drain the excess oil on a paper towel and leave to cool.

To Serve

Place a spoonful of risotto in the middle of your plate and sit the beef on top. Add a little of the leftover mixed wild mushrooms for garnish on top of the beef. Place 3 baby turnips and 3 cep mushrooms around the risotto before drizzling the red wine jus around and garnish with crispy wild rocket.

PAN-FRIED DORSET LAMB

WITH A MINI SHEPHERD'S PIE, ROSEMARY AND
GARLIC ROASTED ROOT VEGETABLES AND REDCURRANT JUS

 45 minutes   Serves 4   Oven 180°c

Chef's comments

This is one of my classic original recipes, combining modern and traditional techniques.

Ingredients

2 lamb loins

For the vegetables
8 garlic cloves (skin on)
4 rosemary sprigs
1 turnip
1 swede
1 carrot
2 celery sticks
1 celeriac
1 parsnip

For the shepherd's pie
100ml lamb stock
200g minced lamb
2 potatoes (mashed)
4 thyme sprigs
1 onion
1 carrot
50g peas

For the garnish
4 redcurrant sprigs
200ml lamb jus

Method

For the shepherd's pie – finely dice the onion and carrot, sweat in a little olive oil, add the minced lamb and season. Add the lamb stock and peas, cook for 10 minutes. Grease a small tian ring, half fill each ring with the mixture. Pipe mashed potato on top and garnish with a sprig of thyme. Place in a medium hot oven for 10 minutes until the mashed potato is golden brown.

Peel all the vegetables and cut each vegetable into different shapes. Blanch separately in boiling water. Roast all of the vegetables in a little olive oil and butter with garlic cloves and rosemary sprigs.

Season the lamb and seal in a pan on both sides with a little olive oil. Place in a warm oven for around 8 minutes or until the lamb is cooked to your taste.

To Serve

Place the shepherd's pie at the top of the plate, carefully removing the tian ring. Add a selection of the roasted vegetables at the bottom of the plate.

Slice each lamb loin into 12 pieces. Place 6 slices of lamb on top of the root vegetables. Warm the redcurrants up in the lamb jus. Once warm, place on top of the lamb loin. Pour a little jus around the lamb and shepherd's pie.

ROAST SUPREME OF CORN-FED CHICKEN

FILLED WITH FETA CHEESE AND SUN-BLUSHED TOMATOES
WITH PESTO MASH AND ROSE HARISSA JUS

 GF

 30 minutes   Serves 4   Oven 180°c

Chef's tip

By stuffing the chicken breast with cheese, tomatoes and basil – it stays moist in the middle during cooking.

Ingredients

4 chicken breasts
100g feta cheese
16 sun-blushed tomatoes
Fresh basil (chopped)
Thyme

For the pesto mash
200g mashed potatoes
2 tbsp pesto

For the garnish
1 tbsp Rose Harissa paste
150ml red wine jus
150g green beans (blanched)

Method

Mix the feta, sun-blushed tomatoes and 2 tablespoons of chopped basil together. Season and seal the chicken on both sides in a hot pan. Carefully make a hole in the chicken. Stuff the chicken with the mixture, place into an ovenproof dish, add some fresh thyme and cook in the oven for 15-20 minutes.

Bring the red wine jus to the boil and add the Rose Harissa.

Heat up the mashed potatoes, add the pesto, some basil and a little olive oil. Toss the green beans in butter and season.

To Serve

Place a spoonful of pesto mash in the middle of each plate, add the green beans on top. Slice the chicken breast in half lengthways, place on top of the beans. Pour a little red wine jus around the chicken, garnish with the roasted thyme.

Brookfield Farm
HIGH WELFARE MEATS

QUALITY
STANDARD
beef
British

BEEF EN CROUTE

ROAST BEEF WITH SPINACH AND WILD MUSHROOMS WRAPPED IN
PUFF PASTRY WITH POMME PURÉE, GREEN BEANS AND MADEIRA SAUCE

 60 minutes   Serves 6   Oven 180°c

Chef's comments

An amazing dish for dinner parties. Prep the day before to make this an easy dish and still enjoy your dinner party – a no stress showstopper!

Ingredients

1 large beef fillet
2 pancakes
250g spinach (cooked)
100g mixed mushrooms (cooked)
1 puff pastry sheet
1 egg
Dried herbs
Poppy and sesame seeds

For the chicken mousse
100g skinless chicken breast
100ml double cream
1 egg
Basil, parsley & tarragon

For the garnish
200ml red wine jus
250g cooked green beans
400g pomme purée (mashed potatoes)

Method

Place the chicken breast into a blender, season and blend for 2 minutes. Add the egg, then slowly add the double cream. Place into a bowl and add some freshly chopped herbs and cooked wild mushrooms.

Season the beef and seal on both sides. Lay the puff pastry on a clean surface, placing the pancake on top. Add the dry, cooked spinach on top and then spread over the chicken mousse to cover the spinach. Place the sealed beef fillet in the middle.

Carefully roll the pastry around the fillet of beef and seal the two ends with egg wash. Decorate with puff pastry leaves and other decorations if you wish.

Season and sprinkle over the dried herbs and seeds, place on a lined baking tray and bake for 30 minutes. If the pastry starts to go dark, cover with foil and continue cooking.

The temperature in the middle of your beef en croute should be 34°c for medium rare. Remove from the oven and leave to rest for 15 minutes. Carefully slice your beef en croute into 6 slices.

To Serve

Place a spoonful of pomme purée at the top of the plate with the green beans on top. Balance the beef fillet at an angle over the pomme purée and beans. Drizzle with red wine jus and serve the remaining in a jug on the side.

QUALITY STANDARD lamb British

SLOW-BRAISED LAMB SHOULDER

WITH CONFIT CARROTS, BABY TURNIPS, MINTED MASH AND LAMB JUS

 4 hours
 Serves 8
 Oven 160°c

Chef's comments

This is a great winter dish. Braising the meat means it's very tender and falls off the bone.

Ingredients

1 lamb shoulder (boned)
1 onion
2 garlic cloves
1 leek
1 large carrot
3 litres of lamb stock
Rosemary & thyme sprigs

For the minted mash
750g potatoes
(Maris Piper or King Edward)
50g butter
3 mint sprigs (finely chopped)

For the garnish
500g carrots
250ml goose fat
24 baby turnips
500g curly kale
500ml lamb jus

Method

Place the lamb shoulder in a deep tray, season and add the roughly chopped onion, garlic, leek and carrot. Cover with lamb stock, add the rosemary and thyme and braise in the oven for around 4 hours or until you are able to flake the meat.

Remove from the tray, removing any skin or fat and flake the meat onto some cling film. Roll into a large sausage shape and cut into 8 slices.

Wash the potatoes and place in a pan of boiling water (skin on) and simmer for 15 minutes until cooked. Peel and mash until smooth with the butter and stir in the mint.

Peel the carrots and chop into rustic pieces, place into a pan with some thyme and cover with the goose fat. Cook for 20 minutes until soft, drain.

Peel and cook the baby turnips for 6 minutes in boiling salted water, drain and toss in a little olive oil. Sauté the curly kale in a little butter and season well. Warm the lamb jus.

To Serve

Place a large spoonful of mint mash in the middle of each plate, add some curly kale and then a piece of lamb shoulder, arrange 3 baby turnips and 6 carrots around the plate. Pour the sauce over the meat.

OVEN-BAKED PORK CUTLET

TOPPED WITH THINLY SLICED HAM AND SWISS CHEESE SERVED WITH
SAUTÉED POTATOES, CREAMED CABBAGE, SAGE AND CIDER JUS

 45 minutes Serves 4 Oven 180°c

Chef's tip

Take a humble pork chop and by simply adding the flavours of ham and cheese, it creates an amazing dinner the whole family will enjoy!

Ingredients

4 pork cutlets
4 thin ham slices
4 Swiss cheese slices

For the vegetables
800g cooked new potatoes
600g Savoy cabbage
2 carrots (peeled)
150ml double cream

For the garnish
12 cherry apples
500ml red wine jus
150ml cider
1 rosemary sprig
4 sage sprigs

Method

Pan-fry the pork cutlets with the sage on both sides then place into the oven for 5 minutes. Remove from the oven, turn the cutlets and top with the ham and cheese. Oven cook for a further 5 minutes until the pork is cooked through and the cheese is melted. Remove the cutlets and place the pan back on the hob, add the cider and reduce by half. Add the red wine jus and the cherry apples.

Slice the potatoes into circles and shallow-fry in olive oil with the rosemary for 5 minutes, turn when needed. Season and drain.

Finely slice the cabbage, blanch for two minutes in boiling salted water, drain and sweat in a saucepan with a little olive oil. Grate the carrots and add seasoning. Mix well, add the double cream and continue to cook until the cream has reduced.

To Serve

Arrange the sautéed new potatoes in the middle of each plate, spoon the cabbage on top, place 1 cutlet on top of the cabbage and 3 cherry apples around, pour the cider jus over and garnish with the sage.

STEAK AND CHUNKY CHIPS

WITH WATERCRESS AND SHALLOT SALAD AND A HP JUS

 45 minutes Serves 4

Chef's tip

Adding a little bit of HP Sauce to the jus enhances the flavour and works really well with steak and chips.

Ingredients

4 sirloin steaks (6oz each)
8 red-skinned potatoes

For the jus
1 tbsp HP sauce
100ml red wine jus

For the garnish
200g watercress
1 shallot (cut into fine rings)
10ml extra virgin olive oil

Method

Peel and cut the potatoes into chunky chip shapes (roughly 7cm x 1.5cm). You'll need 6 chips per person. Blanch in salted water for 5 minutes then drain, dry and deep fat fry at a low temperature for 5 minutes. Once the chips are soft, remove, turn the fryer to full heat and re-fry until golden brown and crispy. Drain and season.

Season your steak and drizzle with olive oil. Chargrill in a hot pan for approximately 4 minutes on each side or until the steak is cooked to your taste.

Meanwhile, heat the red wine jus in a saucepan. Once hot add the HP sauce and stir in.

To Serve

Mix the watercress with the shallot and some olive oil, place on the top corner of each plate. Add 6 chips and the steak, top with the sauce.

ROAST LOIN OF VENISON
WITH A FIG AND RED ONION TARTE TATIN

 40 minutes   Serves 4   Oven 190°c

Chef's comments

Venison is one of the leanest meats available and therefore requires very little preparation.

Ingredients

1 venison loin (24oz)

For the tarte tatin
2 figs (cut in half)
2 red onions
1 bay leaf
200ml red wine
150g puff pastry
20g butter
20ml Acacia honey

For the sauce
200ml venison/beef stock
100ml red wine
2 juniper berries
50g shallots (sliced)
25g celery (sliced)
25g button mushrooms (sliced)
Thyme

For the garnish
12 baby turnips
10g black trumpet mushrooms
250g runner beans

Method

For the sauce – sauté the trimmings from the venison until brown. Add the sliced mushrooms, celery, shallots and thyme. Add the red wine and reduce by half, add the stock and reduce by half again. Pass through a sieve and season.

To make the tarte tatin – peel the onion and cut in half, cook in the red wine until soft and drain. Leave to cool before removing the middle of the onion and replacing with a fig half.

Roll the puff pastry out until ½ cm thick, cut out 4 circles just larger than the onions and wrap each onion in the puff pastry. Do not cover the fig. Line 4 Yorkshire pudding moulds with greaseproof paper, add 5g of butter and 5ml of honey to each. Place the onion on top, fig side down. Cook for 10 minutes.

Season the venison and cut into 4 pieces, seal in a hot pan and then roast in the oven for 10 minutes, remove, leave to rest and then slice into 5.

Cook the turnips in some boiling salted water with a little sugar for approximately 8 minutes or until just soft. Drain, toss and season in butter. Slice the trumpet mushrooms into julienne, toss and season in butter. Slice the runner beans into julienne, blanch in salted water then toss and season in butter.

To Serve

Place some runner beans in the middle of each plate, place the onion and fig tarte tatin on top (fig facing up). Place 3 turnips around the outside, the mushroom on top of the turnips and the sliced venison on top of the tarte tatin. Pour over the sauce.

Brookfield Farm
HIGH WELFARE MEATS

QUALITY
STANDARD
beef
British

BROOKFIELD ROAST FILLET OF BEEF

WITH POMME PURÉE, CEP MUSHROOMS, CRISPY PANCETTA AND BABY CARROTS

 45 minutes   Serves 4   Oven 180°c

Chef's comments

Being the QSM Ambassador, I am a huge advocate for good quality meat. Fillet is one of my favourite cuts of beef.

Ingredients

4 beef fillets (6oz each)

For the vegetables
12 baby turnips (peeled)
12 baby cep mushrooms
12 baby carrots (peeled)

For the garnish
3 slices of pancetta
200g pomme purée
(mashed potatoes)
2 celery sticks (chopped)
¼ butternut squash
50g curly kale
150ml rod wino jus
5g sugar
10g butter to season

Method

Peel the squash and the celery, cut into 1cm cubes. Blanch in salted water for approximately 5 minutes before draining. Drizzle with olive oil and roast in the oven for 10 minutes until golden brown and soft.

Place the pancetta between 2 sheets of greaseproof paper on a baking tray, weigh down with another tray to keep the pancetta flat. Oven cook for 6 minutes until the pancetta is golden brown. Remove from the oven and allow to cool and crisp.

Place the turnips in a saucepan with cold water, a little salt and the sugar. Bring to the boil and simmer for 10 minutes. In another saucepan, add the carrots and celery, cold water and salt. Simmer for around 5 minutes. Separately toss the carrots, celery and turnips in butter and season.

Wash and pan-fry the mushrooms in olive oil until soft. Season to taste and then cut each one in half. Wash and sauté the curly kale in olive oil before seasoning to taste.

Season and pan-fry on both sides to seal the beef. Place in the oven for approximately 6 minutes for medium rare, longer for different preferences.

To Serve

Pipe the pomme purée into a twist in the middle of the plate and a ball on one side of the plate – garnish with the curly kale, butternut squash and celery. Slice the beef in half and arrange one half on top of the purée and the other on the side of the plate – sprinkle with sea salt. Arrange the carrots, turnips, mushrooms and pancetta around the plate and then drizzle the red wine jus.

ROAST RUMP OF LAMB
TOPPED WITH A CRANBERRY CRUST

WITH SAUTÉED POTATOES, SAVOY CABBAGE AND GLAZED CHESTNUTS

 60 minutes   Serves 4   Oven 180°c

Chef's comments

This is a great autumnal dish using seasonal ingredients.

Ingredients

4 lamb rumps (8oz each)
100g fresh breadcrumbs
50g cranberries

For the vegetables
4 small carrots
200ml goose fat
1 small Savoy cabbage
100g celeriac
20 new potatoes
1 garlic clove
Rosemary & tarragon

For the garnish
12 chestnuts
200g sugar
120g green beans (blanched)
1 tomato
50g butter
150ml red wine jus

Method

Blend the cranberries and breadcrumbs for 1 minute, until the breadcrumbs turn red. Season and seal the lamb on both sides, add some rosemary and oven cook for 7 minutes. Top with the breadcrumbs and return to the oven for a further 7 minutes.

Make the sauce by cutting the tomato into quarters, remove the seeds and dice. Bring the jus to the boil, add the diced tomato and a small amount of chopped tarragon.

Thinly slice the cabbage and the celeriac. Blanch both in salted water for 3 minutes, drain and toss in butter. Cook the potatoes, drain and slice, roast in butter with garlic and rosemary.

Peel, chop and cook the small carrots in a little goose fat for approximately 20 minutes. Check seasoning.

Cook the sugar with 200ml water until it forms a golden brown syrup. In another pan, simmer the chestnuts for 20 minutes or until soft. Drain, cool and add to the syrup, simmer for 15 minutes. Remove chestnuts and boil the syrup, add the chestnuts back into the pan and simmer for 10 minutes or until the chestnuts are coated. Leave them in the syrup.

To Serve

Place the potatoes in the middle, add some cabbage, top with the green beans. Slice the lamb into 5 slices and place on top of the cabbage. Add the carrots and chestnuts around the lamb. Pour over the sauce.

La Chasse
Hunter gathering for chefs
www.lachasselimited.co.uk

SLOW-ROASTED SUPREME OF DUCK

WITH PARSNIP PURÉE, PARSNIP CIRCLES, GREEN BEANS AND BLACKBERRY JUS

 45 minutes   Serves 4   Oven 180°c

Chef's tip

The secret to cooking duck is allowing it to rest for at least 5 minutes otherwise it will have a rubbery, tough texture.

Ingredients

4 duck breasts
4 slices of foie gras
120g green beans (blanched)

For the parsnip circles
8 parsnip circles (1cm thick)
100g butter

For the parsnip purée
200g parsnips (peeled)
100g potatoes (peeled)
10ml double cream
200ml milk

For the jus
100ml duck/red wine jus
12 blackberries

Method

Seal the duck breasts on both sides. Roast in the oven for 3-4 minutes each side with some rosemary. Once cooked, leave to rest for 5 minutes. Pan-fry the foie gras slices for 2 minutes on each side.

Meanwhile, to make the parsnip circles, season and then seal on both sides in a pan before placing into an ovenproof dish. Half cover with water and the butter. Place into the oven and cook for 10-15 minutes or until the parsnips are cooked.

Cut the potatoes and parsnips into 1cm cubes. Add to the milk in a saucepan and bring to the boil, cook until soft (roughly 15 minutes). Drain the vegetables, return to the pan with the double cream and heat through. Blend until smooth and season to taste.

Toss the green beans in a little olive oil. Warm the blackberries in the jus and keep on a low heat until ready to serve.

To Serve

Place the parsnip purée in the middle of the plate, add the tossed green beans on top. Place 2 parsnip circles next to the beans. Slice the duck breast and place on top and add the foie gras. Finish by pouring over the jus and arrange the blackberries.

ROAST LOIN OF ENGLISH VEAL

WITH WATERCRESS PURÉE, OXTAIL AND MARMITE RAGOUT, BABY CARROTS, MUSHROOM GRATIN AND RED WINE JUS

 4.5 hours Serves 4 Oven 180°c

Chef's comments

Marmite is one of my favourite ingredients, adding a couple of spoons when braising the oxtail enhances the flavour.

Ingredients

1 veal loin (24oz)

For the oxtail

400g oxtail

2 red onions

6 peppercorns

½ bunch thyme

2 celery sticks

2 carrots

4 garlic cloves

2 litres of beef stock

½ bunch rosemary

2 tsp of Marmite

40g breadcrumbs

For the potatoes

4 potatoes

100ml double cream

20g wild mushrooms

For the vegetables

200g curly kale

8 baby carrots

8 baby turnips

100g watercress

100g leeks (finely sliced)

10g unsalted butter

For the garnish

160ml red wine jus

Method

Cut the 2 onions in half and roast in the oven for 10 minutes. Remove and keep the 2 outer layers. Trim the oxtail and place in a deep tray with the carrots, celery, peppercorns, thyme, garlic, rosemary and the remaining onion. Cover with the stock and cook for 4 hours at 170°c until tender. Once cooked remove from the liquid. Take the meat off the bone, flake, season and add the Marmite. Take some of the sauce and reduce to a syrup, mix through the oxtail. Fill the 4 onion rings with the mixture, top with breadcrumbs and oven cook for 5 minutes, until the breadcrumbs have turned golden brown.

Slice the mushrooms and soften in a pan. Peel and finely slice the potatoes. Mix with the double cream, thyme, mushrooms and season. Layer into an ovenproof dish. Cook for 45 minutes until soft and golden brown. Turn out and cut into 4 slices.

Soften the leeks, add the watercress, cook for 1 minute. Season and blond.

Trim and seal the veal in a hot pan. Oven cook at 180°c for 8 minutes (medium rare). Rest for 10 minutes then slice into 20.

Peel and blanch the baby vegetables in salted water for 5 minutes. Once cooked, drain and toss in a little butter with the curly kale.

To Serve

Place the mushroom gratin at the top of the plate, make a swipe on each plate with the watercress purée. Place the oxtail onion on top, arrange the baby vegetables, add the curly kale and then place 5 slices of veal on top. Pour over some red wine jus.

ROAST SUPREME OF GUINEA FOWL

FILLED WITH APRICOTS AND SERVED WITH CONFIT LEG,
GRATIN POTATOES, CURLY KALE AND RED WINE JUS

 2 hours   Serves 4   Oven 150°c

Chef's tip

Stuffing the guinea fowl with apricots adds a sweetness to the dish.

Ingredients

2 whole guinea fowl
500ml goose fat
1 rosemary sprig
2 thyme sprigs
8 fresh apricots
1 orange (halved)

For the potatoes
4 large potatoes
2 garlic cloves (chopped)
300ml double cream

For the garnish
500g curly kale
2 carrots (peeled & grated)
500ml red wine jus

Method

Remove the legs and breast from the guinea fowl, place the legs into an ovenproof dish with 1 thyme sprig, rosemary, orange and seasoning. Cover with goose fat and cook in the oven for 90 minutes. Drain and cut each leg into 2 pieces – drumstick and thigh.

Wash, peel and thinly slice the potatoes, season and mix with the double cream, garlic and thyme, layer the potatoes in an ovenproof dish and bake at 150°c for 60 minutes, remove from the oven and cut into 4.

Remove any skin or bones from the thighs and flake the meat into a bowl. Add 6 apricots, roughly chopped, mix well. Pan-fry the breasts on both sides. Remove and make a hole in each breast, fill with the thigh and apricot mixture. Increase the oven temperature to 180°c and cook for 9 minutes. Turn halfway through and add the drumsticks.

Finely slice the kale, blanch for 2 minutes in boiling salted water, drain and add to a saucepan, sweat with a little oil. Add the carrots, season well and mix. Cook for 2 minutes.

Warm the red wine jus. Cut the remaining two apricots into 6 wedges each, pan-fry for 1 minute on each side.

To Serve

Arrange the gratin potato at the top of the plate, place 3 apricot wedges on top of each potato, follow with a large spoonful of kale at the bottom of the plate. Slice the guinea fowl supreme in half and arrange on the kale, stand 1 drumstick next to the potato, pour the jus around.

MINI ROAST 'CANNON' OF BEEF

WITH MINI YORKSHIRE PUDDINGS, PARSNIP PURÉE AND A RAGOUT OF BABY VEGETABLES

 45 minutes   Serves 8   Oven 180°c

Chef's comments

A posh and smaller version of the traditional Sunday roast. It's a lighter and more refined take on this classic.

Ingredients

2 beef cannons/sirloins
(24oz each)
1 onion
1 carrot
2 rosemary & thyme sprigs

For the Yorkshire puddings
100g plain flour
¼ tsp salt
3 eggs
175ml milk
4 tbsp vegetable oil

For the parsnip purée
750g parsnips
100ml double cream

For the seasonal vegetables
Baby turnips, baby carrots, asparagus, green beans, baby corns

For the garnish
750ml red wine jus

Method

Seal the beef in a hot pan on all sides. Slice the onion and carrot and lay on a roasting tray, add the cannon, drizzle with oil, season, add the rosemary and thyme. Oven cook for 15-18 minutes for medium rare, remove and leave to rest for at least 10 minutes.

For the Yorkshire puddings – turn the oven up to 220°c. Mix the flour and salt together in a bowl, add the eggs and a little milk, mix well and then slowly whisk in the remaining milk until you get a nice smooth mixture, pour the mixture into a jug.

Place a teaspoon of vegetable oil into 16 small muffin tray holes, transfer to the oven and leave for 5 minutes or until the oil is piping hot. Carefully remove the tray from the oven and pour the Yorkshire pudding batter into the holes. Cook for 15 minutes or until golden brown and well-risen. (These can be made in the morning and then re-heated in the oven for a few minutes before serving).

To make the parsnip purée – peel and chop the parsnips, cook in boiling salted water for 12 minutes, drain and blend with the warm double cream, season to taste. Peel and cook the baby vegetables, once cooked drain and toss in olive oil. Warm the red wine jus.

To Serve

Cut each cannon into 16 thin slices. Swipe a spoonful of parsnip purée across each plate, place 4 slices of beef on one side of the parsnip purée, place 2 mini Yorkshire puddings on the other side, arrange a nice selection of vegetables next to the Yorkshire puddings and pour over the red wine jus, serve a jug of extra jus on the side.

Fine dining at Stoke Park

Humphry's.

AUTUMN ROASTED LOIN OF VENISON

WITH PARSNIP PURÉE, CHARRED BRUSSELS SPROUTS, CRANBERRY COMPOTE, GAME CHIPS AND VENISON JUS

 45 minutes   Serves 4   Oven 180°c

Chef's tip

Cranberry and venison are not a classic combination but they complement each other really well.

Ingredients

1 venison loin (24oz)

For the parsnip purée
1kg of parsnips
15ml double cream
15ml milk
10g salted butter

For the compote
100g cranberries
20g sugar
100ml red wine

For the garnish
1 King Edward potato
50g curly kale
6 baby turnips
100g Brussels sprouts
8 chestnuts
10g honey
150ml venison/red wine jus

Method

Season and seal the venison, oven cook for 5 minutes for medium rare. Peel the turnips and add to a pan with cold water, some salt and 5g sugar. Boil for 10 minutes until soft. Drain, season and toss in butter. Sauté the curly kale with oil and season.

Peel and roast the chestnuts for about 8 minutes. Mix with honey and caramelise in the oven for a few minutes. To make the compote, place the cranberries, 15g sugar and red wine in a saucepan. Bring to the boil and simmer for around 15 minutes until jam like.

Peel the parsnips, slice 2 very thinly with a mandolin, deep-fry for 30 seconds. Drain on a paper towel. Leave to cool and crisp up.

Dice remaining parsnips and simmer in a saucepan with the milk, cream and a little salt for roughly 20 minutes until soft. Drain, keeping the milk and cream in a jug. Blend parsnips, slowly add the butter, milk and cream until you create a smooth consistency.

Blanch the sprouts in salted water for 5 minutes. Drain before halving and frying in a pan until they become golden brown. Peel the potato and slice on a mandolin. To create the criss-cross effect, rotate the potato 90 degrees before each slice. Deep-fry for 2 minutes until golden brown. Drain and allow to cool and crisp up. Slice the venison into 8.

To Serve

Swipe the parsnip purée across the plate, place 2 piles of curly kale on either side. Place 2 slices of venison on top. Arrange the turnips, chestnuts and sprouts around the plate. Dollop the cranberry compote, garnish with chips and parsnip crisps. Serve the warm jus in a jug.

QUALITY
STANDARD
lamb
British

ROAST LAMB CUTLETS

WITH A RAGOUT OF PEAS AND BEANS, COCOA AND CHILLI JUS

 20 minutes   Serves 4   Oven 180°c

Chef's comments

This is a Moroccan-style bean ragout with a Wheeler twist – the cocoa is the hidden ingredient.

Chef's tip

The cocoa and chilli mix can be rubbed on the cutlet for the perfect barbecue dish.

Ingredients

12 lamb cutlets
3 rosemary sprigs

For the ragout
35g cocoa powder
2 red chillies
100g chickpeas (cooked)
100g cannellini beans (cooked)
100g red kidney beans (cooked)
100g peas
1 small red onion
1 garlic clove
1 carrot

For the garnish
12 orange cherry tomatoes
400ml lamb jus

Method

Finely chop the red onion and garlic, sweat in a pan with a little olive oil. Add all the beans and peas, cook for 2 minutes, add half the lamb jus and simmer for 8 minutes.

Finely chop the red chillies and mix with the cocoa powder, sprinkle this mixture on both sides of the lamb cutlets, pan-fry the lamb cutlets on both sides for 3 minutes with the rosemary. Remove from the pan and allow to rest for 3 minutes.

Leave the pan on the heat and add the remaining lamb jus to the pan, simmer for 3 minutes. Place the cherry tomatoes on a baking tray, season and sprinkle with olive oil, place under the grill for 2 minutes.

To Serve

Place a large spoonful of the bean mixture in the middle of each plate, place 3 lamb cutlets on top of the beans and arrange 3 cherry tomatoes around. Pour some of the lamb jus over the cutlets and garnish with the cooked rosemary sprigs.

VEAL MEDALLIONS
WITH FONDANT POTATO, TENDERSTEM BROCCOLI, PURPLE ASPARAGUS AND CAPER JUS

 60 minutes Serves 4 Oven 180°c

Chef's comments

veal is an often over-looked meat but very full of natural flavours and something that I recommend that you should try.

Ingredients

1 veal loin (24oz)

For the potatoes
4 large potatoes
1 rosemary sprig
100g butter
1 litre vegetable stock

For the vegetables
500g tenderstem broccoli
8 purple asparagus spears

For the garnish
8 caper-berries
10g mini capers
500ml red wine jus

Method

Peel the potatoes and cut each potato into a circle using a cutter, pan-fry in a little oil and place in a ovenproof dish. Add the butter, rosemary sprig and the vegetable stock. Cover and place into the oven for 20 minutes – the potatoes should be golden brown and soft in the middle.

Peel the purple asparagus, cut in half and cook in boiling salted water for 4 minutes, drain and toss in olive oil. Trim the tenderstem broccoli, cook in boiling salted water for 3 minutes, drain and toss in olive oil.

Warm the red wine jus and add the mini capers.

Slice the veal loin into 12 medallions. Season and pan-fry on both sides for 2 minutes. Add a little butter and baste the medallions. Remove from pan.

To Serve

Place 1 fondant at the top of each plate, arrange 2 large caper-berries on top of each potato. Place some purple asparagus and tenderstem broccoli at the bottom of each plate, lay 3 veal medallions on top, pour over some capers and jus.

ASSIETTE OF PORK

SLOW-COOKED BELLY WITH SPICED APPLE JELLY, PAN-FRIED TENDERLOIN WITH SAVOY
CABBAGE, CHIPOLATAS WITH MUSTARD MASH AND CARAMELISED ONION WITH APPLE JUS

 2.5 hours   Serves 8   Oven 160°c

Chef's tip

Make sure you slow-cook the pork belly for maximum effect and by adding mustard to the mash it creates a little kick.

Ingredients

For the chipolatas

16 pork chipolatas
250g mashed potatoes
1 tsp of wholegrain mustard
1 onion

For the tenderloin

4 pork tenderloins
2 thyme sprigs
1 carrot
1 small Savoy cabbage

For the pork belly

500g pork belly
5g ground cinnamon
2 litres of stock
200g curly kale

For the garnish

16 cherry apples
100g spiced apple jelly
750ml red wine jus

Method

Seal the pork belly on both sides and place in a deep baking tray skin side up, sprinkle with sea salt and cinnamon, pour around the stock. Cover and braise in the oven for 2 hours, checking every 30 minutes. Once the belly is cooked, cut into 8 pieces, place under the grill for a few minutes to crisp up the skin.

Pan-fry the tenderloin and place in the oven for 8 minutes, remove from the oven and add the chipolatas and thyme. Cook for 10 minutes until brown, turning halfway through cooking. Leave to rest for at least 5 minutes. Slice each tenderloin into 8.

Finely slice the cabbage, blanch for 2 minutes in boiling salted water, drain and add to a saucepan. Sweat with a little olive oil, grate the carrot into the pan, season and mix well. Cook until the cabbage is soft.

Heal up the mashed potatoes and add the wholegrain mustard, place into a piping bag. Sauté the curly kale in a little butter and season well. Slice the onion thinly and sauté in butter until soft and caramelised. Cut the spiced apple jelly into 16 cubes. Add the cherry apples to the red wine jus and heat through.

To Serve

Place a spoonful of cabbage in the middle, arrange 4 slices of pork tenderloin on top. Pipe the mustard mash on one side of the plate and place 2 chipolatas on the mash, top with some caramelised onions. Place some curly kale on the other side of the plate and top with the pork belly. Arrange 2 squares of spiced apple jelly and 2 cherry apples around the plate and pour over the jus.

ROAST MINI SIRLOIN OF BEEF
WITH 'ONION COTTAGE PIE' AND THYME JUS

 45 minutes   Serves 8   Oven 180°c

Chef's comments

I love cottage pie so I decided to experiment by serving it inside an onion. This is my Dad's favourite dish.

Ingredients

2 beef cannons/sirloins

(24oz each)

1 onion

1 carrot

2 rosemary & thyme sprigs

For the cottage pie

2 red onions

300g minced beef

1 carrot

1 celery stick

1 shallot

1 garlic clove

250g mashed potatoes

250ml red wine jus

For the vegetables

750g green beans

750g curly kale

For the garnish

750ml red wine jus

2 thyme sprigs

Method

Seal the cannons in a hot pan, slice the onion and carrot and lay on a roasting tray, add the cannon, pour over a little olive oil and season. Add the rosemary and thyme and place into the oven 15-18 minutes for medium rare, remove and leave to rest for at least 10 minutes.

For the cottage pie – peel and cut the onion in half. Place on a roasting tray and sprinkle with olive oil, oven cook for 10 minutes until soft, remove from the oven and separate each layer of the onion. Select 8 nice layers and place back on the tray.

Warm up the mashed potato and place into a piping bag with a star nozzle. Finely dice the shallot, garlic, celery and carrot and sweat in a little olive oil, add the minced beef and season well. Add 250ml red wine jus and cook for 15 minutes. Now fill each of the onion layers with the minced beef and pipe the mashed potato on top. Place in a oven for 10 minutes until the mashed potato is a golden brown.

Cook the green beans in boiling salted water for 4 minutes, once cooked drain and toss in olive oil. Sauté the curly kale in water and season. Warm the 750ml red wine jus with 2 thyme sprigs.

To Serve

Cut each cannon into 20 slices. Place the onion cottage pie at the top of each plate and the curly kale at the bottom of the plate add the beans on top of the curly kale and then arrange 5 slices of beef on top. Pour over the red wine jus.

THATCHAM
BUTCHERS

ROAST SUPREME OF CORN-FED CHICKEN

WITH SAGE AND ONION STUFFING, PARISIENNE POTATOES, PANCETTA CRISPS AND GRAPE JUS

 60 minutes   Serves 4   Oven 180°c

Chef's comments

A modern twist on the classic chicken dinner – pan-frying the stuffing adds another dimension to the norm.

Ingredients

4 chicken breasts
2 thyme sprigs

For the stuffing
200g sage & onion stuffing
1 tbsp Branston pickle

For the vegetables
3 large potatoes
8 baby turnips
8 baby carrots
4 baby courgettes
200g green beans
5g butter

For the garnish
4 pancetta slices
4 seedless black grape bunches
500ml red wine jus

Method

Pan-fry the chicken on both sides to seal. Place in the oven with the thyme for 18 minutes, turning halfway through.

Make the stuffing according to packet instructions then stir in the pickle. Roll into a sausage shape and steam for 15 minutes, cool and slice into 8. Pan-fry on both sides for 2 minutes just before serving.

Wash and peel the potatoes and using a melon baller, make 32 small potato balls. Blanch in boiling salted water for 3 minutes, drain and then place into a roasting tray with a little olive oil and the thyme. Season and roast for 8 minutes until the potato balls are golden brown and soft in the middle.

Place the pancetta between 2 sheets of greaseproof paper on a baking tray, weigh down with another tray to keep the pancetta flat. Cook in the oven for 15 minutes. Leave to cool and crisp up.

Peel and cook the baby carrots and baby turnips in boiling salted water for 6 minutes. Slice each baby courgette into 5 pieces and cook in boiling water with the green beans for 3 minutes. Drain all the vegetables and toss in the butter, season well.

To Serve

Warm the red wine jus in a pan and add the bunches of grapes. Cut the chicken into 3 pieces and add a slice of sage and onion stuffing in-between each slice, place at the bottom of the plate. Place 8 potato balls on the top left of each plate, arrange a selection of vegetables at the top right of each plate. Place a bunch of grapes on top of the chicken, pour the red wine jus over and finish with a pancetta crisp.

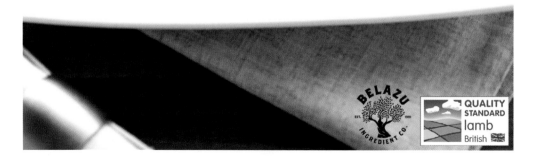

PAN-FRIED LOIN OF LAMB
WITH BRAISED LAMB OSSO BUCCO

SERVED WITH BABY MEDITERRANEAN VEGETABLES AND BLACK OLIVE JUS

 3 hours   Serves 8   Oven 160°c

Chef's comments

You may not be familiar with fregola pasta but don't be afraid to try it!

Ingredients

4 lamb loins
750g fregola
1 litre vegetable stock

For the osso bucco
8 lamb osso bucco slices
(from the shank)
1 carrot
1 celery stick
1 onion
2 garlic cloves
2 rosemary & thyme sprigs
2 litres of lamb stock
100ml red wine
20g plain flour

For the vegetables
4 baby aubergines
4 baby courgettes
4 baby red peppers

For the garnish
750ml lamb jus
30g pitted black olives
(cut into rings)

Method

Seal the slices of lamb osso bucco in a pan, sprinkle with flour and continue cooking for 2 minutes. Place the lamb osso bucco in a deep tray, season and add the roughly chopped onion, garlic, celery and carrot, cover with the lamb stock, red wine and add 1 sprig of rosemary and thyme. Cover and braise for roughly 2 hours or until the meat is very soft.

Season the lamb loins and seal in a hot pan with a little olive oil. Place into the oven for approximately 5 minutes or until the lamb is cooked to your required taste.

Cut the peppers in half lengthways, leaving the stalk on and remove the seeds. Cut the baby aubergines and courgettes in half lengthways, place all the baby vegetables on a baking tray, season, add a drizzle of olive oil and 1 sprig of rosemary and thyme. Cook for 10 minutes, until all the vegetables are soft.

Place the fregola into a pan, season and add the vegetable stock, bring to the boil and simmer for 12 minutes. Warm the lamb jus and add the olives.

To Serve

Slice each loin into 10 pieces. Place a large spoonful of fregola on one side of the plate, lay 5 slices of lamb loin on top, place 1 piece of lamb osso bucco at the top of the plate on the other side, arrange 2 halves of each vegetable at the bottom of each plate, pour over the black olive jus.

VEGETARIAN

Entertaining crowds at one of my favourite events – Taste of London

If Chris isn't hard at work in the kitchens of **Stoke Park** creating culinary masterpieces, you can hear him on the radio, appearing on a number of different channels and shows including *Capital FM, BBC Berkshire* and *Chef Radio,* on topics varying from an insight into his dishes to his views on local produce and developing cooking techniques.

Along with this Chris writes a monthly food column for *The Buckinghamshire Advertiser* showcasing some of his latest recipes.

If hearing him on the radio or reading his articles in the paper wasn't enough, Chris is a familiar face on our TV's appearing on *Hell's Kitchen 2* alongside *Jean-Christophe Novelli* and more recently on BBC1's *Saturday Kitchen*, Channel 4's *Sunday Brunch* and BBC2's *Great British Menu.*

On *Saturday Kitchen,* Chris appeared alongside *James Martin, Jason Atherton* and

Rashida Jones, cooking his signature *Smoked Scallop Niçoise* – a dish with a real theatrical serving.

When reflecting back on his appearance, Chris spoke about his excitement to participate in the *Omelette Challenge* – a *Saturday Kitchen* tradition which saw his face take a permanent spot on the *Omelette Challenge Wall of Fame!*

Chris has appeared on *Sunday Brunch,* rubbing shoulders with *McBusted, Gareth Thomas* and *Susie Dent,* cooking *Pan-fried fillet of Sea bass with Potato Purée, Samphire, Clams and Teign Mussels Nage* for them all to try, let's just say this went down a real treat!

Chris has also appeared on BBC 1's *'Chef's, Put your menu where your mouth is'.*

BAKED AUBERGINE AND
MEDITERRANEAN VEGETABLE 'LASAGNE'
WITH CHARGRILLED ARTICHOKE AND SUN-DRIED TOMATO SAUCE

 45 minutes   Serves 4   Oven 160°c

Chef's comments

I love my mother-in-law's vegetable lasagne so I decided to give it a twist by serving it in an aubergine – it gives this dish the wow factor.

Chef's tip

Make sure that you par cook the aubergine before filling it.

Ingredients

For the lasagne
4 aubergines
2 red peppers
1 green pepper
1 yellow pepper
2 courgettes
2 garlic cloves
1 onion
6 plum tomatoes
100ml tomato juice
4 lasagne sheets
400ml Béchamel sauce
150g mozzarella (grated)
150g wild rocket

For the seasonal vegetables
Carrots, baby corns, baby courgettes, green beans (blanched)

For the sauce
1 shallot
2 button mushrooms
5g saffron
400ml vegetable stock
100ml double cream
100ml white wine

Method

Cut the top off the aubergine and scoop out the inside. Season and drizzle with olive oil. Bake the whole aubergine in the oven for 10 minutes.

Finely dice the peppers, onion, garlic, courgettes and plum tomatoes. Sweat in a little olive oil and season.

Add the tomato juice and cook to form a ratatouille. Blanch the pasta sheets. Build your lasagne inside the aubergine – ratatouille, pasta, Béchamel sauce, grated mozzarella and repeat until aubergine is full. Place back into the oven for 15 minutes.

Toss the seasonal vegetables in a little butter.

Make the saffron sauce by slicing the shallot and mushrooms and sweat in a little olive oil, add the saffron and the white wine, add the vegetable stock and reduce by half then add the double cream, check seasoning and pass through a sieve.

To Serve

Place the aubergine in the middle of the plate. Top with a little fresh rocket. Place the aubergine lid back on top of the lasagne. Display the seasonal vegetables around. Pour over the sauce and serve.

PUMPKIN WELLINGTON

WITH GREEN BEANS AND TRUFFLE MASH

 60 minutes   Serves 4   Oven 180°c

Chef's tip

Use pancakes to stop the pastry from going soggy and bake on a wire rack – this allows the air to circulate and avoids a soggy bottom!

Ingredients

For the Wellington
1 large pumpkin
4 pancakes
400g mixed mushrooms
200g brie (sliced)
500g spinach (cooked)
1 puff pastry sheet
1 egg yolk
100g mixed herbs (chopped)
4 rosemary sprigs
1 garlic clove

For the truffle mash
4 Maris Piper potatoes
20ml double cream
10g black truffle shavings

For the sauce
250ml vegetable stock
1 onion

For the garnish
400g green beans (cooked)

Method

Peel and cut the pumpkin into chunks and roast in the oven with rosemary, olive oil, garlic and seasoning for 20 minutes until the pumpkin is soft. Once cooked, allow to cool and remove the rosemary and garlic.

Blanch the spinach for 30 seconds in boiling salted water then cool, drain and dry. Wash the mushrooms then roughly chop into large chunks. Pan-fry in olive oil and season. Once soft, leave to cool.

Lay the puff pastry sheet out whole and cover with the pancakes then layer with spinach. Place the pumpkin chunks on top (save ¼ for the sauce) and sprinkle with the herbs, cooked mushrooms and add the sliced brie.

Egg-wash the border of the pastry. Then roll to form a sausage shape. Egg-wash the outside of the Wellington, season with salt and pepper. Place on a wire rack and bake for 18 minutes at 180°c until golden brown.

Peel and cook the potatoes. Drain, mash and season with the double cream and butter, remembering to add hot cream and butter to the potatoes to avoid lumps. Add the truffle shavings.

Warm the beans and season. Slice and sweat the onion in a pan. Add the remaining cooked pumpkin. Cover with vegetable stock. Simmer for 10 minutes then blend, pass through a sieve and check seasoning to form a sauce.

To Serve

Carefully slice the Wellington and lay at an angle on top of the quenelle of potato alongside the beans. Pour the sauce around.

GLOBE ARTICHOKE 'TARTLET'

FILLED WITH WILD MUSHROOMS AND SPINACH,
CARROT AND SWEET POTATO BOULANGÈRE AND SAFFRON SAUCE

 60 minutes   Serves 4   Oven 180°c

Chef's comments

A lovely combination of spring and summer flavours make this a great seasonal dish.

Ingredients

For the tartlet
4 globe artichokes
1 lemon (juiced)
100g flour
1 litre vegetable stock
400g spinach
400g mixed wild mushrooms
Basil, tarragon & chives
1 puff pastry sheet
1 egg yolk

For the boulangère
2 sweet potatoes
1 medium onion
6 carrots
500ml vegetable stock

For the sauce
1 shallot
2 button mushrooms
5g saffron
400ml vegetable stock
100ml double cream
100ml white wine

Method

Trim the outside leaves of the artichokes. In a pan place the stock and flour, mix well. Add the artichoke and lemon juice and simmer for 30 minutes until the artichoke is soft. Remove from the pan and scoop out the middles, trim the heart. Blanch the spinach in boiling water for 30 seconds, cool and drain.

Roughly chop the mushrooms and sweat with 50g mixed herbs. Place a quarter of the spinach inside the artichoke hearts. Top with the cooked mushrooms.

Cut pastry into 4 squares, egg wash the artichoke and carefully cover with the pastry, egg wash again. Oven cook for 18 minutes.

Peel and thinly slice the carrots and sweet potatoes. Peel and thinly slice the onions, sweat. Add the carrots and sweet potatoes. Cover with stock and oven cook for 15 minutes until the stock is absorbed. Whilst still warm, place into 4 metal rings.

To make the sauce – slice the shallot and mushrooms and sweat in a little oil. Add the saffron, white wine and vegetable stock. Reduce by half. Add the cream, check seasoning and pass through a sieve.

To Serve

Place the artichoke tart at one end of the plate and the boulangère potatoes at the other end of the plate. Drizzle with saffron sauce.

WILD MUSHROOM RISOTTO
SERVED WITH ROCKET AND BASIL OIL

 45 minutes   Serves 4

Chef's comments

This dish is quick and easy to prepare – my kids love it – so I highly recommend it as a family favourite!

Ingredients

For the risotto
500ml mushroom stock
10g herbs
1 garlic clove (chopped)
1 onion (diced)
600g risotto rice
40ml white wine
600g wild mushrooms
Pinch of mixed spice
40g mascarpone
150g vegetarian Parmesan
Knob of butter

For the garnish
200g wild rocket
Basil oil

Method

Boil the mushroom stock with the herbs. In another large pan add the garlic clove and onion, cook for 5 minutes.

Add the risotto rice to the onion and garlic, coat with olive oil. The oil will prevent the rice from sticking together. Pour in the white wine and the mushroom stock, cook for 15 minutes, keep stirring the rice. Add the pinch of ground mixed spice to give the dish a kick.

Meanwhile, sauté the wild mushrooms and season. After 5 minutes, add ¾ of the cooked wild mushrooms, grated Parmesan, butter and mascarpone to the risotto. Season to taste.

To Serve

Ladle the risotto into large bowls and top with the rocket, remaining mushrooms and season. Drizzle with basil oil.

DOUBLE-BAKED
DORSET BLUE VINNY CHEESE SOUFFLÉ

WITH APPLE, BEETROOT AND THYME SALSA

 20 minutes   Serves 4   Oven 175°c

Chef's comments

Beetroot and apple accompany the cheese perfectly and bring a sweetness to the dish. You can enjoy this as a starter, main course or even a dessert!

Chef's Tip

You can swap the strong blue cheese for any cheese of your choice – goat's cheese, or a strong cheddar.

Ingredients

For the soufflé

450ml milk

2 fresh bay leaves

80g butter

100g plain flour

200g Dorset Blue Vinny Cheese

50g vegetarian Parmesan (grated)

6 egg yolks

6 egg whites

250ml double cream

For the salsa

1 cooked beetroot

1 Granny Smith apple

10g chives (chopped)

10g thyme (chopped)

40ml extra virgin olive oil

5ml cider vinegar

For the garnish

60g baby salad

600g cooked new potatoes

100g wild rocket

8 baby golden beetroot

1 candy beetroot

Method

Make a roux with the flour and the butter. Slowly add the milk and double cream. Add the bay leaves and Dorset Blue Vinny Cheese. Cook out, cool slightly and whisk in the egg yolks. Remove ¼ of the mixture (this will be used for glazing later).

Butter 4 ramekins and sprinkle with the grated Parmesan. Whip the egg whites to form soft peaks. Carefully beat the egg whites into the mixture. Fill your ramekins. Place in the oven for 10-12 minutes until golden brown and well-risen.

For the salsa – finely dice the cooked beetroot and apple. Mix with the chives, thyme, vinegar and oil. Season to taste.

Slice the new potatoes and sauté in a little olive oil. Peel and blanch the golden baby beetroot and toss in a little olive oil. Peel and thinly slice the candy beetroot and place into iced water.

To Serve

Arrange the sautéed potatoes in the middle of the plate, add some seasoned wild rocket. Place the warm Dorset Blue Vinny Cheese soufflé on top. Display the salsa around the soufflé and garnish with the baby golden beetroot, baby salad and sliced candy beetroot.

Chef of the Year

BERKSHIRE AND BUCKINGHAMSHIRE LIFE FOOD AND DRINK AWARDS

SUN-BLUSHED TOMATO, BRIE AND BASIL RAVIOLI

WITH ROASTED CHERRY TOMATO COMPOTE AND PURPLE PESTO

 45 minutes   Serves 8   Oven 180°c

Chef's tip

Ravioli is a very delicate pasta so be careful not to pierce when cooking.

Ingredients

For the ravioli
800g pasta flour
7 eggs
1 tsp tomato purée

For the filling
500g brie
200g sun-blushed tomatoes
50g purple basil

For the compote
500g cherry tomatoes
2 garlic cloves
1 shallot
1 rosemary sprig
1 red pepper

For the purple pesto
200g purple basil
100g vegetarian Parmesan cheese
100g toasted pine nuts
100ml extra virgin olive oil

For the garnish
150g baby salad
75g pine nuts
24 orange cherry tomatoes
Micro-cress

Method

To make the ravioli – mix the flour, tomato purée and eggs until they form a dough. Chop the brie and sun-blushed tomatoes, add the basil and season.

Roll out the dough very thinly, keeping it covered with cling film. Cut out 6cm diameter circles and place some filling on half of the circles. Brush the edges with water and top with an empty pasta circle. Seal and make 3 folds in each. Cook in salted boiling water for 4 minutes.

For the compote – finely slice the shallot, red pepper and garlic. Cook with some olive oil and half the cherry tomatoes. Add the herbs to the pan and cook for 15 minutes. Season to taste.

To make the pesto – place all ingredients into a blender and blend until smooth.

Toast the pine nuts under the grill for a few minutes until golden brown. Roll the orange cherry tomatoes in olive oil, season and grill for 3 minutes.

To Serve

Place a large spoonful of tomato compote in the middle of each plate, place 3 ravioli on top. Spoon the pesto around, sprinkle the pine nuts, garnish with the orange cherry tomatoes, micro-cress and remaining purple basil leaves.

PUMPKIN AND WALNUT GNOCCHI
WITH PUMPKIN PURÉE, TOASTED PINE NUTS AND WILD ROCKET

 2 hours Serves 6 Oven 180°c

Chef's comment

Gnocchi made from scratch is a good comfort food and also a fun one to make with the family. Adding pine nuts gives a little crunch!

Chef's tip

Pan-fry the gnocchi to give a nice crisp texture and golden colour. Using the pumpkin purée in the dough gives it an unusual colour.

Ingredients

For the gnocchi

1kg potatoes
(Maris Piper or King Edwards)
3 eggs (beaten)
300g plain flour
500g pumpkin
1 rosemary sprig
75g walnuts (chopped)
15g butter

For the garnish

60g pine nuts
250g wild rocket
60g vegetarian
Parmesan shavings
10g micro-basil

Method

Peel the pumpkin and cut 100g into 1cm cubes. Roughly chop the rest, keep the trimmings. Roast in the oven with some olive oil and rosemary for 15 minutes or until soft. Keep the cubes to one side. Blend the remainder into a purée. Wash and spin dry the rocket. Place the pine nuts on a baking tray and place under the grill to toast until golden brown.

Wash and boil the potatoes (skin on) until just soft, remove from the pan once cooked and peel quickly, mash until smooth. Make a hole in the middle of the potatoes and add 3 tablespoons of pumpkin purée, the walnuts, eggs and sprinkle over some of the flour. Mix with your hands, adding more flour as you go. Try to add as little as possible, as you want the potato flavour and not flour! Work carefully and quickly, as the more you handle the dough, the harder and bouncier it will become.

Roll into long sausage shapes, cut into 3cm lengths, roll in a little flour and imprint on one side with the back of a fork.

Boil a large pan of salted water and drop the gnocchi in to cook for 2 minutes (do not try to cook them all at the same time). They should bob to the surface. Once they are cooked, scoop them out with a slotted spoon and dry on a tea towel. Once they are all cooked, pan-fry in a little butter with the cubes of pumpkin until they are golden brown on all sides.

To Serve

Swipe a spoonful of the pumpkin purée across each plate, add 8 pieces of gnocchi and a few pumpkin cubes around, add a few drops of pumpkin purée around the plate and garnish with the micro-basil, top the gnocchi with wild rocket and Parmesan shavings.

BUTTERNUT SQUASH, SPINACH AND VEGETABLE COUSCOUS FILLED CANNELLONI
WITH BABY PROVENÇALE VEGETABLES AND BUTTERNUT SQUASH EMULSION

 40 minutes   Serves 4   Oven 180°c

Chef's tip

This is a great dish to cater for all allergies – just be sure to buy gluten-free alternatives of the ingredients.

Ingredients

For the cannelloni
8 gluten-free lasagne sheets
250g gluten-free couscous
½ red, green & yellow pepper
1 courgette
250g spinach
1 large butternut squash
1 garlic clove
2 rosemary sprigs

For the vegetables
4 baby aubergines
4 baby red peppers
16 broccoli florets (blanched)
4 marinated artichokes

For the sauce
1 onion
400ml vegetable stock

For the garnish
Micro cress

Method

Peel and slice the squash into long batons, keeping all the trimmings. Place everything onto a baking tray, season and add the rosemary, garlic and olive oil, roast for 15 minutes until soft.

Finely chop the peppers and courgette, sweat in a pan, add the couscous and 250ml of vegetable stock. Simmer for 5 minutes.

Sauté the spinach in olive oil, season and drain. Blanch the lasagne sheets in boiling water, drain. Lay out the lasagne sheets and cover with the cooked spinach, 2 pieces of butternut squash and then 4 spoonfuls of the vegetable couscous. Roll up the lasagne sheets and wrap in cling film, steam for 10 minutes.

Cut the baby vegetables and artichokes in half lengthways. Leave the stalk on the peppers and remove the seeds. Place all the vegetables on a baking tray with a sprig of rosemary and thyme, drizzle with olive oil and season. Cook for 10 minutes, until soft.

Slice the onion and sweat in a saucepan, add all the remaining butternut squash and cook for 2 minutes. Blend until smooth, remove half the purée and place into another pan, add 150ml of stock to the pan and blend again to make an emulsion. Toss the broccoli in olive oil.

To Serve

Swipe a spoonful of the thick butternut purée across each plate, add a spoonful of couscous. Remove the cannelloni from the steamer, unwrap and place in the middle. Arrange the vegetables around the cannelloni, pour some of the emulsion over and garnish with the micro-cress.

TRUFFLE MACARONI CHEESE STUFFED TOMATO

WITH A MIXED SEED AND PARSLEY TOPPING

 40 minutes Serves 8 Oven 180°c

Chef's comments

Adding truffle oil to your traditional macaroni cheese enhances the flavour and the richness of the tomato.

Ingredients

For the macaroni
8 beef tomatoes
800g macaroni
400g cheddar cheese (grated)
50g butter
50g plain flour
500ml milk
10ml truffle oil
200g parsley (finely chopped)
100g panko breadcrumbs
100g mixed seeds
(sunflower, pumpkin, chia)

For the garnish
24 purple asparagus
80ml extra virgin olive oil

Method

For the Béchamel – place the milk into a pan, add the butter and flour, bring to the boil, stirring all the time, once it starts to thicken add the grated cheese, truffle oil and seasoning.

Cook the macaroni in boiling salted water for 12 minutes (or as per packaging) drain and mix with the Béchamel.

Remove the top of the beef tomatoes, using a spoon carefully scoop out the insides, season and fill with the macaroni cheese. Blend 50g of the parsley with the extra virgin olive oil.

Toast all the seeds under a grill for a few minutes, mix with the parsley and breadcrumbs, sprinkle over the top of the macaroni, place into the oven for 10 minutes.

Peel and cook the purple asparagus in boiling water for 4 minutes, drain and toss in a little olive oil.

To Serve

Place 4 pieces of asparagus in the middle of each plate, carefully add the beef tomato on top and drizzle with a little parsley oil.

DESSERTs

It is Chris' flexibility as a chef which makes him legendary at *Stoke Park.*

Away from the kitchen, Chris recreated the Olympic torch as an exquisite cake to celebrate London 2012, he even ran the London Marathon (twice!) dressed as a chef. The first whilst flipping pancakes and the second carrying a 10kg stockpot.

Chris' values run deep with cooking for the homeless on Christmas Day, donating himself for cook-off's and charity master-classes.

All of this is not done in vain – tens of thousands of pounds has been raised for numerous charities.

Away from his hectic work life, Chris is at home with his wife and twin daughters. When asked who does the cooking at home, his answer is… his wife! Why you may ask? Because he uses every pot and pan in the kitchen!

WHOLE BAKED APPLE CRUMBLE
WITH POACHED BLACKBERRIES AND DORSET GINGER CUSTARD

 45 minutes   Serves 4   Oven 180°c

Chef's tip

My mum makes an amazing apple crumble – I have experimented by adding
Dorset Ginger with cinnamon – enjoy!

Ingredients

For the apple compote
4 whole apples (Braeburn)
50g sugar
Cinnamon

For the crumble
250g unsalted butter
125g sugar
250g plain flour

For the custard
10ml Dorset Ginger
Cinnamon
250ml double cream
125g egg yolk
65g sugar

For the blackberries
100g blackberries
50g sugar

For the garnish
4 vanilla ice cream scoops

Method

Cut the top off the apples and carefully remove the insides with a spoon. Keep the insides for later. Place the whole apples upside down on a baking tray and cook for 10 minutes until slightly soft.

Meanwhile dice the apple insides and place into a pan on a low heat, add the sugar and a pinch of cinnamon to create the compote.

Mix all crumble ingredients together to form a breadcrumb. Place on a lined baking tray and cook in the oven until golden brown. Once cooked and cooled, break up with a fork.

For the custard – boil the cream and milk together and mix the egg yolk with the sugar. Once boiling, slowly stir the eggs and Dorset Ginger into the cream mix.

To poach the blackberries – boil the sugar and 50ml water. Remove from the heat and place blackberries into this mix. Leave to cool down, the blackberries will cook in the mix as it cools.

Place the apple compote inside the whole apple and top with the crumble mix. Cook before serving for another 10-15 minutes to heat through. Dust with icing sugar.

To Serve

Put some custard in the middle of the plate. Place the apple on top and a scoop of ice cream on the side. Decorate with the poached blackberries. Extra custard can be served in a jug.

CHRIS WHEELER'S HUMPHRY'S BAR

WITH HAZELNUT-PRALINE FILLED WAFERS AND CARAMEL ICE CREAM

45 minutes   Serves 8

Chef's comments

Created alongside Reece Collier, a great friend, this is an adaptation of one of our fine-dining restaurant Humphry's dishes.

Ingredients

Bahlsen hazelnut-praline
filled wafers
8 peanut caramel bars
(Snickers or Chris Wheeler's)

For the Anglaise
500ml milk
500ml double cream
250g egg yolk
125g sugar

For the chocolate mousse
310ml Anglaise
2 gelatine leaves
240g milk chocolate
310ml whipping cream

For the garnish
8 caramel ice cream scoops
80g salted peanuts (blitzed)
80g milk chocolate (melted)

Method

Bring milk and cream to the boil. Meanwhile mix the egg yolks with the sugar. Once boiling, slowly add the egg mixture. Take off the heat and pass through a sieve. This is the Anglaise.

For the chocolate mousse – soak the gelatine in cold water, squeeze out excess and dissolve into the warm Anglaise. Add the chocolate and allow to melt. Mix well. Leave to cool. In the meantime, whip the cream to soft peaks and fold into the cooled chocolate mix. Leave to set.

To Serve

Best served on a long rectangular plate. Make a small pool of melted chocolate and brush across the plate. Add 2 quenelles of the mousse.

Cut the peanut bars into 3 and place next to the mousses. Cut each wafer in half and place 3 pieces on the plate. Sprinkle some blitzed peanuts on top of the mousses. Create a small pile of peanuts and top with ice cream.

PIMM'S SUMMER PUDDING

WITH CLOTTED CREAM

 20 minutes   Serves 8

Chef's comments

Pimm's and clotted cream are the epitome of great British summertime so combine them both to make this perfect summery pudding.

Ingredients

For the pudding
16 slices of white bread
1kg frozen berries mix
500g raspberry purée
500g sugar
1 vanilla pod
100ml of Pimm's

For the garnish
4 clotted cream scoops

Method

Place the raspberry purée in a pan with the sugar. Bring to the boil and add the frozen mixed berries. Stir on a low heat for another 5-10 minutes until softened but not completely cooked.

Remove from the heat and add the Pimm's. Leave to cool, keeping the sauce for soaking the bread and the berries separate.

Cut 1 circle and 1 rectangle from each slice of bread. Soak 1 bread circle and place into the bottom of your mould. Soak the 2 rectangles and push into the sides of the mould, creating a circular edge. Fill with the berries mixture and place another soaked round on top. Repeat for each ramekin.

Cling film tightly and place in the fridge to cool for at least 4 hours.

Sieve the leftover liquid used for soaking and use it to pour over the pudding and for decorating the plate.

To Serve

Remove the pudding from the mould, place in the middle of the plate and arrange additional sauce, berries and clotted cream around.

MILK CHOCOLATE AND SALTED PEANUT PARFAIT
WITH WARM CARAMEL SAUCE

 45 minutes   Serves 8

Chef's tip

This dish was created alongside my friend and Stoke Park's pastry chef Sarah Edwards. She says, 'pour the sauce around the parfait for your guests at the table to give a wow factor!'

Ingredients

For the parfait
2 eggs
125g caster sugar
500ml double cream
100g milk chocolate
75g salted peanuts (blitzed)

For the garnish
200ml caramel sauce
80g milk chocolate
Icing sugar

Method

Melt the chocolate in a bain-marie. Whip the eggs and sugar to a sabayon over a pan of warm water until light and fluffy.

Slowly add the melted chocolate. Lightly whip the double cream and fold into the mixture. Pour into 4 mousse rings and place in the freezer to set. Leave in the fridge to set for at least 2 hours.

Warm the caramel sauce in a saucepan and keep on a low heat until ready to serve.

To Serve

De-ring your parfaits. Temper the 80g of milk chocolate and pour ¼ onto a cool marble slab, spread it out, trim the edges and carefully wrap it around your parfait and fold the top to form a present like shape. Repeat this 3 more times.

Place 1 parfait in the middle of each bowl. Dust with icing sugar. Pour the warm caramel sauce into a jug.

MOSSY'S SWEET YOGURT AND COCONUT MOUSSE DOME

WITH A RASPBERRY CENTRE AND BITTER CHOCOLATE SHAVINGS

 20 minutes

 Serves 4

Chef's comments

When you cut this dessert, your guests will have a nice surprise seeing the raspberry centre.

Ingredients

For the raspberry centre
40g raspberry purée
10g sugar

For the dome
475g Mossy's Sweet Yogurt
45ml milk
7 gelatine leaves
120g sugar
465g whipping cream
Vanilla essence
150g coconut purée

For the salsa
1 passion fruit
½ mango
½ papaya
1 kiwi
¼ pineapple

For the garnish
50g dark chocolate

Method

Boil the raspberry purée with the sugar. Using a small dome shaped mould, fill halfway and freeze. Keeping 10g aside for the garnish.

Mix the yogurt with the sugar and vanilla essence. Soak the gelatine into cold water. Pour the milk into a pan and heat up. Boil the milk and coconut purée. Dissolve the gelatine into the milk and slowly pour into the yogurt mixture.

Whip the cream by hand until it forms soft peaks and fold into the yogurt. Pour into a dome mould halfway and insert the raspberry frozen half dome inside, fill with more yogurt mixture and freeze.

Remove from the mould once frozen so that you have a smooth finish. Defrost before serving.

Melt some chocolate and spread onto acetate sheets, cut out triangles and use it as a decoration on the dome.

For the tropical fruit salsa – half and scoop out the seeds from the passion fruit. Peel and dice the mango, papaya, pineapple, kiwi and mix with the passion fruit.

To Serve

Place a dome in the middle of the plate. Decorate with the chocolate triangles. Arrange raspberry purée dots and tropical fruit salsa around.

EARL GREY AND VANILLA CRÈME BRÛLÉE
WITH PEACH ICED TEA SORBET

 45 minutes   Serves 4   Oven 135°c

Chef's comments

Serving this crème brûlée in a teacup adds a little 'Mad Hatter' theme. The iced tea works really well as a sorbet.

Ingredients

For the sorbet
600g peach purée
(blitzed and sieved fruits)
300ml loose leaf Newby Earl Grey Tea
300ml water
300g sugar

For the crème brûlée
400g egg yolk
200g sugar
1litre double cream
40g loose leaf Newby Earl Grey Tea

For the garnish
8 biscotti biscuits

Method

To make the sorbet – boil everything together and churn it in an ice cream machine until soft, smooth and ready to serve.

Boil the cream with the Earl Grey Tea. Combine sugar and yolks. When the cream is boiling add the egg mixture to the cream, pass it through a fine sieve. Pour into tea cups and cook in a bain-marie for 35-40 minutes or until firm to the touch.

To Serve

Sprinkle sugar on top and caramelise under the grill or with a blow torch, top with the sorbet. Place 2 biscotti biscuits on the side.

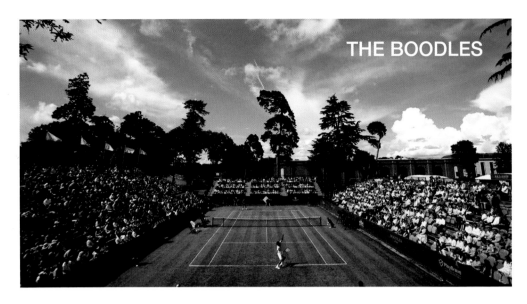

THE BOODLES

"I love cooking at The Boodles as they always give me such flexibility to create amazing dishes for their well-informed and discerning guests."

Chris' ability in creating exquisite fine dining food for large events is always showcased at **The Boodles,** *Stoke Park's* annual tennis event, where he cooks for 800 hospitality guests every day over 5 days.

A reviewer for *A Luxury Travel Blog* summed it up by commenting: *'This is mass catering of Michelin star quality and can only be described as a triumph.'*

Cooking at *The Boodles* event, this 5 day tennis challenge, which is in its 17th year, and takes place at the end of June every year, sees Chris and his team plate up just under 9,000 delicious Three-course Lunches and Afternoon Teas.

At *The Boodles* Chris likes to pull out all the stops from producing edible tennis balls that when served are complete with grass court and net, to getting the waiting staff to serve tennis ball truffles on tennis rackets.

BOODLES
1798

ASHOKA®

ALWAYS A STORY

CHAPTER 2018 | ALL THE RIGHT MOVES

BOODLES
1798

'BOODLES' TENNIS BALL
WITH MASCARPONE CHEESECAKE
WITH DIGESTIVE BISCUIT CRUMBLE AND LIME JELLY

 45 minutes   Serves 6

Chef's comments

This is a dish I created especially for the much-loved 'The Boodles' event that is the showpiece of Stoke Park's summer season. The thousands of people who attend always rave about its presentation and taste – I hope you will love it as much as they do!

Ingredients

For the tennis ball
12 Valrhona white chocolate domes
60g Valrhona white chocolate
40g cocoa butter
1 tsp yellow food colouring

For the tennis net
50g Valrhona white chocolate

For the cheesecake
500g mascarpone
175g icing sugar
175g yogurt
4 gelatine leaves
150ml milk
500g double cream

For the lime jelly
250ml lime juice
75g sugar
75ml water
4 gelatine leaves
Drop of green food colouring

For the garnish
250g digestive biscuits
24 raspberries

Method

Melt the chocolate and place in a piping bag, draw a tennis net onto a sheet and leave to set.

To make the cheesecake – soak the gelatine in cold water. In the meantime mix the mascarpone, icing sugar and yogurt together. Warm the milk in a pan, add the gelatine and dissolve. Pour into the mascarpone mixture and fully incorporate. Leave to one side, whip the cream until it forms a soft peak and fold into the mascarpone mix. Pipe into 6 dome moulds, leaving 1cm empty at the top. Leave to set in the fridge.

For the lime jelly – soak the gelatine in cold water. Boil the sugar, water and juice together. Once boiling, remove from the heat, dissolve the gelatine and add green food colouring. Leave to cool then pour on top of the cheesecake layer. Leave to set. Once set, place a net in the centre of the jelly.

Melt the white chocolate to use as a glue to stick the 2 halves together (1 filled and 1 empty) and create the ball. Refrigerate to set and remove from the mould.

Mix the cocoa butter with the yellow food colouring and using a paint spray gun, colour the balls yellow. Pipe white chocolate lines on the ball to create the full tennis ball effect.

To Serve

Blitz the biscuits to create a crumb and sit the ball on top, the crumb stops the balls from sliding. Decorate with raspberries.

Bahlsen

CHOCO MOMENTS CRUNCHY MINT BISCUIT AND RASPBERRY 'MILLE FEUILLE'

WITH RASPBERRY SORBET

 45 minutes   Serves 4

Chef's comments

This is my twins, Vittoria and Vanessa's favourite dessert and it's very simple to make so it's good for a family day of fun, creating and then eating this dish together.

Ingredients

Bahlsen dark chocolate
and mint biscuits
500g raspberries

For the raspberry cream
250ml double cream
50g mascarpone
50g blitzed fresh raspberries
50g sugar

For the Chantilly cream
250ml cream
50g sugar
Vanilla essence

For the raspberry coulis
250g raspberries (blitzed to a purée)
125g sugar

For the garnish
4 raspberry sorbet scoops
8 mint sprigs

Method

Make the raspberry cream by mixing together the mascarpone, sugar and raspberries. Whip the cream and fold into the mascarpone mixture. Refrigerate.

Meanwhile make the Chantilly by whipping together the cream, sugar and vanilla essence.

For the coulis – boil the purée and in a second pan boil the sugar with a bit of water. Once boiling, place the sugar in with the purée. Boil again, remove from the heat and leave to cool.

To Serve

Decorate the plate with the raspberry coulis. Place the 2 creams into piping bags. Place a small amount of cream directly onto the plate and lightly press a biscuit on top to stick it to the plate.

Top the biscuit with 3 raspberries and then pipe dots of both creams on top. Place another chocolate biscuit on top and finish with a scoop of sorbet and a mint sprig.

'BANANA-RAMA'

BANOFFEE PIE, BANANA AND VANILLA CRÈME BRÛLÉE, BANANA TARTE TATIN WITH RUM AND RAISIN ICE CREAM

 90 minutes   Serves 12   Oven 135°c

Chef's comments

I created this dish whilst in the Dominican Republic drinking Piña Coladas.

Ingredients

For the crème brûlée
450ml double cream
150ml banana purée
125g sugar
8 egg yolks
1 vanilla pod

For the tarte tatin
12 baby bananas
12 puff pastry squares
60g sugar

For the banoffee pie
200ml condensed milk
75g butter
75g dark brown soft sugar
3 bananas
100ml whipped cream
25g grated chocolate
12 sweet pastry cases

For the ice cream
75g raisins
15ml dark rum
1 litre double cream
60g glucose
14 egg yolks
350g sugar
12 small brandy snaps

For the garnish
Raspberry coulis

Method

For the crème brûlée – split the vanilla pod lengthways into 4. Boil the purée, cream and vanilla. Whisk the sugar and egg yolks together, add to the boiling cream mixture. Pass through a sieve. Pour into 12 ramekins and cook in a bain-marie for 30-35 minutes or until firm to the touch. Allow to cool, sprinkle sugar on top and caramelise under the grill or with a blow torch.

For the tarte tatin – peel the baby bananas and increase the oven temperature to 180°c. Slowly cook the sugar with a small amount of water on a low heat until a caramel forms (about 10 minutes). Wrap ¾ of the banana in puff pastry. Pour the caramel onto a non-stick baking tray and place the banana face down into the caramel. Bake for 15 minutes or until golden brown.

To make the banoffee pie – place the butter and sugar in a saucepan over a low heat, stirring constantly, until the sugar has dissolved. Add the condensed milk and bring to the boil for about a minute, stirring continuously until a thick golden toffee is formed. Thinly slice the bananas and layer on the bottom of each pastry case. Pour the toffee on top, add another layer of bananas, dust with icing sugar and caramelise. Pipe the whipped cream and sprinkle with grated chocolate.

For the ice cream – soak the raisins in the rum and boil the cream with the glucose. Whisk the yolks and sugar together. Slowly pour on the cream mix, whisking well. Return to the pan and simmer, stirring until it thickens (do not boil). Strain and leave to cool. Churn in an ice cream maker until soft, smooth and ready to serve. Then fold in the soaked raisins.

To Serve

Pipe dots of raspberry coulis on each plate. Place the tarte tatin followed by the brandy snap basket which is filled with a scoop of ice cream. Add the banoffee pie and the crème brûlée.

DORSET MINT CHOCOLATE FONDANT
WITH ORANGE SAUCE AND VANILLA ICE CREAM

 45 minutes   Serves 8   Oven 180°c

Chef's tip

The important thing to remember is to not overcook this dish. The middle is meant to be runny so don't be alarmed if it doesn't spring back to the touch.

Ingredients

For the fondant mix
5 egg yolks
5 eggs
125g sugar
250g butter
250g Dorset mint chocolate
50g flour

For the orange sauce
4 oranges
50g sugar

For the ice cream
600ml milk
600ml double cream
250g egg yolk
125g sugar
4 vanilla pods split in half

For the garnish
4 chocolate straws

Method

To make the fondant – melt the butter and chocolate together until completely combined. Whisk the sugar with the eggs and yolks then stir into the chocolate mixture. Fold in the flour slowly to prevent lumps. Pour the mixture into greased mini pudding moulds and refrigerate.

To make the ice cream – place the milk and cream into a pan. Halve the vanilla pods lengthways and add to the pan. Bring to the boil. Whisk the egg yolks and sugar together until light and fluffy. Pour a third of the cream mixture into the egg, whisking constantly. Then whisk in the remaining two thirds.

Add this mix back to the pan and stir over a low heat until it thickens. Cool over iced water then churn in an ice cream maker until soft, smooth and ready to serve. Ensure you do not overchurn! Place into a freezerproof container and freeze.

Zest 2 of the oranges and juice all 4. Place into a saucepan with 50g sugar and cook until a syrup is formed (about 15 minutes).

Cook the puddings for 8 minutes and serve straight away, do not overcook as the centre should be soft.

To Serve

Make a swipe on the plate with the orange sauce, tip out the fondant into the centre of the plate, serve with a scoop of ice cream, and decorate with chocolate straw.

RHUBARB AND GINGERBREAD SOUFFLÉ

WITH POACHED RHUBARB, GINGER AND RHUBARB SORBET

 45 minutes Serves 8 Oven 180°c

Chef's tip

Make sure you fold the soufflé mixture – do not whip it!

Ingredients

For the soufflé base
500g frozen rhubarb
(boiled and blitzed as a purée)
125g sugar
25g cornflour

For the soufflé
240g egg whites
100g sugar
300g rhubarb soufflé base

For the gingerbread
140g golden syrup
140g black treacle
110g light brown sugar
110g butter
225g self-raising flour
5g mixed spice
5g ground ginger
2 eggs
30ml milk

For the poached rhubarb
100g fresh rhubarb (cut into 2 cm)
50g of sugar

For the sorbet
500g frozen rhubarb
(boiled and blitzed as purée)
150g sugar
Pink food colour if needed
10g grated fresh ginger

Method

For the soufflé base – boil the rhubarb purée and sugar, mix the cornflour with cold water and add to the purée once boiling.

To make the gingerbread – melt syrups, sugar and butter, stir in dry ingredients, add eggs and milk. Mix well. Bake for 40 minutes in a bread tin. Once cool cut half into small pieces and crumb the remaining.

Once cooked, blitz 250g of the cooked gingerbread cake into breadcrumbs. Fold 200g into the soufflé mix and keep 50g aside for decorative crumble.

Poach the rhubarb by boiling the sugar and 50ml water together then place the rhubarb on a low heat and cook until soft. Leave to cook and drain.

For the sorbet – boil the rhubarb purée with the ginger, set aside. In another pan boil the sugar with 150ml water. Combine both mixtures together, if necessary add a drop of food colouring. Pass through a sieve and churn in an ice cream maker until soft, smooth and ready to serve.

For the soufflé – whip the egg whites and sugar together until soft peaks form. Fold in the rhubarb base and pieces of gingerbread. Pour into pre-lined ramekins. Sprinkle the gingerbread crumb on top and cook for 8 minutes.

To Serve

Use a long plate, place 4 pieces of poached rhubarb and gingerbread crumb to the right.

Just before the soufflés are cooked, place the sorbet on top of the rhubarb. Sprinkle the soufflé with icing sugar just before serving.

The Daily Telegraph voted Stoke Park one of...
"...Britain's Best Afternoon Tea"

STOKE PARK
★ ★ ★ ★ ★

CHERRY LAYERED CHEESECAKE 'LIGHTHOUSE'
WITH WHITE CHOCOLATE CHOCO BISCUIT ICE CREAM

 45 minutes Serves 10

Chef's comments

Cherry is a great flavour and we've had a bit of fun changing the shape of the cheesecake – still a simple one to make.

Ingredients

For the cheesecake
Bahlsen dark chocolate biscuits
100g butter
500g soft cream cheese
175g icing sugar
175g crème fraîche
3 gelatine leaves
100g blitzed cherries (purée)
200g white chocolate (melted)
500ml whipping cream

For the ice cream
Bahlsen white chocolate biscuits
10 vanilla ice cream scoops

For the garnish
Bahlsen orange chocolate biscuits
10g white chocolate
1 tbsp mango purée
10 cherries

Method

Soak the gelatine in cold water, squeeze out excess moisture before dissolving into the melted white chocolate.

Mix together the cream cheese, icing sugar and crème fraîche. Fold in the white chocolate, whip the cream and fold into the mixture.

Divide the cheesecake mix into 2, fold the blitzed cherries into half.

Blitz the dark chocolate biscuits with melted butter. Place on a lined baking tray and cut 10 circles out. This will form the bases for the cheesecakes.

Using tin foil individual Christmas pudding moulds, line them with cling film. Layer the white chocolate cheesecake followed by the cherry cheesecake, repeat until almost full. Top with the biscuit circles, leave to set. Blitz the orange biscuit Bahlsen.

Crush the white chocolate biscuits and fold into the vanilla ice cream.

To Serve

Create a white chocolate wave across the plate and then use the blitzed orange biscuits to create sand. Build a "sand castle" with the mango purée and tip out your lighthouse cheesecakes and place a cherry on top. Balance a chocolate biscuit against the cheesecake and then place the ice cream on a mound of crumbled biscuit.

CHOCOLATE AND COFFEE DELICE

WITH CARAMELISED WALNUT, COFFEE SAUCE AND HONEY YOGURT ICE CREAM

 45 minutes Serves 10

Chef's comments

Cooking with coffee and chocolate gives a grown-up flavour. A great one for the coffee lovers.

Ingredients

For the delice

6 egg yolks

2 eggs

200g sugar

350g dark chocolate

50g blitzed walnuts

2 Cafe Du Monde espresso shots

400g double cream

100g Tims Dairy Honey Yogurt

For the chocolate glaze

150ml water

360g sugar

300g cream

130g glucose

8 gelatine leaves

120g cocoa powder

For the caramel sauce

75g sugar

50ml double cream

For the walnuts

30 walnut halves

200g sugar

200ml water

For the garnish

10 honey yogurt sorbet scoops

Method

Place the sugar and a bit of water in a pan and bring to the boil. Melt the chocolate. Whisk the eggs with an electric whisk and once boiling, pour the sugar into the eggs and whisk until cold.

Meanwhile mix the melted chocolate with the coffee and walnuts. Once the egg mixture is completely cold, fold into the coffee mix. Leave to cool.

Whisk the cream until it forms soft peaks and fold the chocolate into it. Add the honey yogurt and mix again. Pour into a tray and leave to set. Once set, cut into 3cm x 9cm rectangles and freeze.

To make the glaze – soak the gelatine, boil all the ingredients except the cocoa powder. Add the gelatine and cocoa powder, remove from the heat. Leave to cool. Once cool, remove the delice from the freezer and place on a rack. Glaze and leave to set in the fridge.

Make the caramel sauce by cooking the sugar and once it is light brown, slowly add the cream and boil until the caramel is dissolved.

For the walnuts – boil the sugar and water, add the walnuts to the boiling syrup. Simmer for 5 minutes. Strain the walnuts and place on a baking tray and cook in the oven on the lowest temperature until dried and candied.

To Serve

On a long plate, make a small pool of sauce and swipe across the plate with the back of a spoon. Place the delice in the middle and decorate with 3 walnut halves and dot the caramel sauce around. Finish with a scoop of honey yogurt sorbet.

BAKED PINEAPPLE TARTE TATIN

WITH COCONUT SORBET AND EXOTIC FRUIT SALSA

 45 minutes   Serves 8   Oven 180°c

Chef's comments

This vegan dessert will impress your guests, using Caribbean summer flavours which complement each other well.

Ingredients

For the tarte tatin
1 medium pineapple
100g sugar
1 puff pastry sheet

For the salsa
½ pineapple
2 kiwis
1 papaya
1 dragon fruit
2 passion fruits

For the sorbet
500g coconut purée/coconut milk
50g sugar
50ml water

For the garnish
50ml mango purée

Method

Make a caramel with the sugar and pour into the tatin moulds. Trim the pineapple and remove the core. Cut into 8 rings. Put the pineapple into the moulds and top with a puff pastry disk (the same size as your mould).

For the salsa – dice all the ingredients and mix together. Refrigerate until needed.

To make the sorbet – boil the water and sugar together, pour in the coconut purée or coconut milk and churn in an ice cream maker until soft, smooth and ready to serve.

To Serve

Cook the tarte tatin just before serving until the pastry is a light brown colour. Place some salsa and mango purée on the plate with the tarte in the middle. Top with the coconut sorbet.

CHOCOLATE ORANGE TART
WITH WHITE CHOCOLATE ICE CREAM

 1.5 hours   Serves 8   Oven 180°c

Chef's comments

This was created with my good friend Stephanie Hakesley who loves the flavours of chocolate and oranges.

Chef's tip

Baking blind involves covering the base of your pastry with cling film or greaseproof paper filled with 'baking beans' (an alternative being rice). This weighs down the pastry and prevents it from rising during the par cooking.

Ingredients

For the sweet pastry
250g unsalted butter
180g sugar
Pinch of salt
2 eggs
500g flour

For the chocolate filling
300g Felchlin dark couverture/chocolate 75%
1 egg
100ml milk
250ml double cream
Zest of 1 orange

For the garnish
8 white chocolate ice cream scoops
10g Felchlin dark couverture/chocolate 75%
8 chocolate butterflies to garnish
Orange purée
2 digestive biscuits

Method

Cream the butter and sugar together, add the eggs, flour and salt. Leave to rest for about 30 minutes. Roll out to a 5mm thickness and place in a tart ring or mould. Bake blind and cook until the sides become light brown. Remove the 'baking beans' and cook until the inside is light brown. Leave to cool.

To make the chocolate filling – boil the milk and cream. Remove from the heat, stir in the chocolate until it's all melted. Lightly beat the egg with the orange zest and add to the chocolate mixture.

Lower the oven temperature to 150°c and cook for 20 minutes.

To Serve

Make a zig-zag across the plate with the dark chocolate sauce adding some random dots with the chocolate and orange purée. Make a crumb with the digestives and balance the ice cream on top. Place the tart in the middle of the plate and decorate with the butterflies.

When I am away from the kitchen, I can always rely on my number two, the amazing Craig Smith.

RED WINE JUS 500ML

Ingredients
50g button mushrooms
1 celery stick
3 banana shallots
1 garlic clove
200ml red wine
1 litre veal/beef stock

Method
Peel and slice the shallots, mushrooms, celery and garlic, sweat in a pan.
Add the red wine, reduce by half, before adding the stock and reducing by half. Season to taste and pass through a sieve.
To make a **lamb jus** – simply use lamb stock instead.

HOUSE DRESSING 500ML

Ingredients
430ml olive oil
50ml Sherry vinegar
10ml honey
10g wholegrain mustard

Method
Whisk the olive oil and vinegar, add the honey and mustard, whisk again, check seasoning and place in an airtight bottle.

BASIC ROUX

Ingredients
40g flour
40g butter

Method
Dissolve the butter in a pan and add the flour. Stir until the mixture forms a smooth paste which leaves the sides and base of pan cleanly. Cook for a minimum of 2 minutes to cook out the taste of the flour.

HOLLANDAISE SAUCE 200ML

Ingredients
125g unsalted butter
2 egg yolks
1 tsp of white wine vinegar

Method
Melt the butter in a saucepan and keep warm. Place the 2 egg yolks, vinegar and seasoning into a bowl and whisk over a pan of simmering water, until the egg yolks become lighter in colour and thick. Slowly whisk in the melted butter. Check the seasoning and serve.

CRÈME PÂTISSIÈRE

Ingredients
4 egg yolks
60g caster sugar
25g plain flour
2 tsp cornflour
280ml milk

Method
Beat the egg yolks and sugar for a few minutes until thick and pale. Whisk in the flours.
Heat the milk in a saucepan until starting to boil. Whisk into the egg mix.

FRUIT BASED SORBET 500ML

Ingredients
300ml fruit purée
100ml water
100g caster sugar
½ lemon

Method
Bring the water and sugar to the boil, add the fruit purée, mix well. Add a squeeze of lemon juice, leave to cool over ice. Once cool churn in an ice cream maker until soft, smooth and ready to serve. Place into a freezer-proof container and freeze.

VANILLA ICE CREAM 1 LITRE

Ingredients
1 vanilla pod (halved lengthways)
500ml full fat milk
500ml double cream
8 egg yolks
180g caster sugar

Method
Place the milk, vanilla pod and cream into a pan. Bring to the boil. Whisk the egg yolks and sugar together until light and fluffy. Pour ⅓ of the cream mixture onto the egg and sugar mixture whisking all the time. Add back into the pan and stir over a low heat until the mixture thickens, cool over iced water. Churn in an ice cream maker until soft, smooth and ready to serve. Place into a freezer-proof container and freeze.

Bain-marie – a pan or tray of hot water in which a cooking container is placed for slow cooking.

Blanch – plunge into boiling water before transferring to iced water.

Caramelise – glaze with sugar to create a crisp topping.

Confit – to cook slowly in oil.

Compote – fruit preserved or cooked in syrup.

Escabeche – a Spanish cooking style where the fish is marinated and cooked in an acidic mixture of vinegar and orange juice and coloured with saffron.

Julienne – to cut vegetables into matchstick shaped pieces.

Pomme purée – a smooth mashed potato.

Quenelle – transferring the contents repeatedly between 2 spoons to create an oval shape.

Ragout – this French comfort food consists of a highly-seasoned combination of slowly cooked ingredients.

Sabayon – whipped and heated egg yolks, sugar, and Marsala wine, served hot or cold.

Terrine – prepared in advance and allowed to cool and set in a container. Served in slices.

Velouté – a creamy soup.

A VERY SPECIAL

Thank You...

Matt Munro – Photographer
studio@mattmunro.co.uk

The King Family – Stoke Park

Karl Pendlebury – Quality Schemes at AHDB Beef and Lamb

Richard and Emma Lamb – Lamb & Wolf Ltd

Editorial Consultant
Stephanie Hakesley

Marketing and PR Consultant **Nick Downie**, Me
and Book Design Consultant **Hayley Walker**

Lara Thorpe – Photographer
www.larajanethorpephotography.com

Maureen McLean – Photographer
www.maureenmcleanphotography.com

Tim Winter – Photographer
www.timwinter.co.uk

Rob Whitrow – Photographer
info@robwhitrow.co.uk

Thank You...

I would personally like to thank all my wonderful suppliers for their support over the many years, and hope they continue supplying me with their amazing ingredients for me to cook!

www.dorset-shellfish.co.uk

www.jurassiccoastmeats.co.uk

www.bahlsen.co.uk

www.brookfieldfarmdorset.co.uk

www.cafedumonde.co.uk

www.creedfoodservice.co.uk

www.classicfinefoods.com

www.dorsetginger.ltd

www.tcfinefoods.co.uk

www.globalfse.co.uk

www.foodspeed.co.uk

www.newbyteas.co.uk

www.sheringhams.com

www.lachasselimited.co.uk

www.onlinebutcher.co

www.timsdairy.co.uk

www.mossysoriginal.com

www.premierfruits.com

www.allisonrisebro.co.uk

www.dbfoods.co.uk

www.kingfisherbrixham.co.uk

www.globalharvestdirect.com

www.belazu.com

DORSET
SEA SALT
CO.

www.dorsetseasalt.co.uk

CHRIS WHEELER

The Ginger Chef 'Served Up'

The Alexander Group
790 Fulham Road
London SW6 5SL
www.thealexandergroup.co.uk
T: 020 7731 7747

Chris Wheeler - Executive Chef
Stoke Park, Stoke Poges
Buckinghamshire SL2 4PG
www.stokepark.com
T: 01753 717171

www.chefchriswheeler.com